How to Build a GPU Mining Rig to Mine
Bitcoin, Monero, Ether, Zcash, and other Cryptocurrenices

Carl Browne

www.snowballpublishing.com

info@snowballpublishing.com

For information regarding special discounts for bulk purchases, please contact Snowball
Publishing at

sales@snowballpublishing.com

Table of Contents

Preface

→ Writing the building GPU mining-rig book

Computing is my hobby. I build computers for fun, sometimes for money, and spend most of my time browsing on eBay or the website of the local second-hand market of electronic devices. How I got into the mining business is interesting. In the summer of 2016, I went to buy a used radiator and pump for my computer. The seller was a student living in a dormitory. I'd noticed a computer in the corner of his room with three MSI Nvidia GTX 970 units. I asked him "Oh, you have a powerful computer over there with three graphics cards, are they in SLI?". He answered, "No, they are not in SLI". I suddenly thought that it might be mining related. I said, "Ah, you have free electricity here in your room; I guess this is a mining rig". He said, "Yeah, how would you know? You must be smart, because nobody said this to me since I moved here!" We chatted for about half an hour and then I went home. Later that day, I started to read around the subject. I knew about Bitcoin mining and that GPUs are as efficient as Bitcoin ASIC miners. Later, I texted him and asked where and how he does the mining. He told me that he mines Ether, not Bitcoin, in a pool of miners. What is a pool? Everything was new and so strange to me and so I became curious. After a week, I built my first GPU mining rig using my Radeon R9 290 card. Fortunately, at the same time, the AMD Radeon 400s series was launched and this was very useful since AMD had not offered any new product for 1–2 years. Later, I placed an order for many Radeon RX 480 graphic cards and continued my GPU mining journey.

On the internet, there is a lot of information about the Bitcoin and Ethereum platforms. Much of the information is about the development of cryptocurrency itself, improving the network efficiency and dealing with real-world problems. As a computer expert, I did a lot of research to obtain a reasonable understanding of how to build a GPU mining computer. It took me 2–3 month and cost me quite a bit of money in experimenting. I learnt by trial and error. In spite of the availability of informative blogs and forums, the information on GPU mining is very scattered and there is very little information on building a GPU mining business. The hardware options are so varied and no one has addressed them all in a blog or article. Also, I could not see any long-term investment calculations and any information on how the mining business would develop.

So, I decided to write some guidelines, a kind of reference booklet covering the many topics that have not been comprehensively addressed elsewhere. In addition to a quick review of cryptocurrency platforms, my intention is to cover the general computer hardware associated with GPU mining and also to give some tips on buying hardware, tips that are hard to find on general mining forums. I also want to discuss such topics as: the heat generated by a mining rig and how this affects the life of the computer components and mining performance; the cost and profit of GPU mining in the short and long term and their variability; and finally, how to build a practical GPU mining rig costing from around $100 up to a multimillion-dollar mining farm.

→ Second revision

I started working on this book in October 2016 and it took me almost six months to complete this first edition. I know it is far from being complete and there are still more topics to cover in a future revision. Also, as my technical expertise is on hardware and how to put the parts together, rather than on software development, most of the information in Chapters 1 and 2, which covers general cryptocurrency and computer hardware knowledge, have been gathered from the web. Moreover, I have tried to write this book in simple English to facilitate understanding. Because English is not my mother tongue, I ask for your understanding if my English at times is not a precise as it should be. I intend to improve the text in the next edition, which I hope will be available by the beginning of the summer of 2017.

However, the price of Ether has increased from $12 of February 2017, to $50 at end of March and to $190 at the end of May. Also, AMD has released two new GPUs of Radeon 570 and 580. As these changes affect the earnings, cost and final profit of a GPU mining rig dramatically, I saw a complete need for a refresh revision on the topics of the book. On the other hand, I feel that step-by-step guide of building a GPU mining rig was not clear enough, so I decided to add an additional Chapter 6 to this matter.

→ Intended Audience

This book is written for those people who have little or no idea about the business of mining cryptocurrencies and how to build a GPU mining rig. The reader does not need to have any prior programming or technical scripting knowledge (a scripting or script language is a programming language that supports scripts). So, it should be suitable for those who regard themselves as "newbies". The topics of heat generation and life of components covered in Chapter 3 and of the earning, cost and investment covered in Chapter 4, are rarely discussed in the context of GPU mining, so these chapters may be of interest even to an expert in the field of mining cryptocurrencies. In the final chapter, I have tried to collect all of the ideas on building a GPU mining rig that I have been able to find on the web and I have put the designs in categories, for instance, chassis with open-air or closed-air designs. The advantages and disadvantages of any particular component or design have been analyzed thoroughly to give the reader as broad a view of the topic as possible.

→ Conventions Used in This Book

In this book, I used some typographical conventions. Text that has been highlighted contains important messages and must be read carefully. A green highlight contains tips or guidelines; a yellow highlight contains a warning. In Chapter 2, buying tips have been separated by lines, and written with contact *width italic*. Hyperlinks in brackets link you to the source of the reference—they are clickable and can be opened by a browser. Underlined text points to an important opinion or fact. Unaltered quotations are given between quotation marks. Also, to avoid confusion, sometimes there is a color connection with two sentences on different lines.

→ Donations and contributions

In writing of this book, I have made considerable use of Wikipedia.com. Some of the material contained on this site may not be totally accurate. I have therefore thoroughly checked all the statistical information. Most of information that I have obtained from Wikipedia or other websites such as Bitcoin Wiki, is related to the definition or explanation of a topic. I have therefore decided to donate 10% of the profits from this book to Wikipedia.com to help them improve their site. I will also give another 5% of the profits to **Zotero** [zoh-TAIR-oh] which is a free, easy-to-use tool to help one collect, organize, cite, and share research sources.

→ Referencing, plagiarism and source links

The citation and referencing in this book has been facilitated by Zotero software. I used the ASME[1] referencing format which I found to be the most useful means of quoting internet references.[2] All of the sources and references used in the preparation of this book are freely available on the web. Also, hyperlinks are added on each of the references on inside the text to ease up following the source link. I would certainly encourage readers to check the material by going to the source of information. Most of the definitions which I used in the book are from Wikipeida.com. For **statistical data and cited facts,** I did not rely on Wikipedia alone

---

[1] ASME is The American Society of Mechanical Engineers.
[2] How is it more informative? In ASME format, the complete address of the web reference is mentioned along with the last access time. Also, inside the text, there is a pair of brackets and a reference number, which is neater and easier to use for someone who reads the text.

but have reconfirmed the data by using other reliable sources. As most of the information in this book relates to the years of 2016 and 2017 and is likely to change quickly, I want to publish it swiftly and to update it from time to time. Many of the purchase links to Amazon or eBay may not available anymore, so these will be refreshed in the next edition of the book; the reader may also be able to find them using the "search phrases and key words". If there is anything in this book that has been copyrighted and I inadvertently had not obtained the right to use it, I will immediately remove it from the eBook once I have been notified.

→ About me!

I am a mechanical engineer. I had wanted to study computers, but unfortunately in the mid-90s, I was given some bad advice. I was asked "What you want to do with a computer degree? Make CDs and sell them! If you want to have a bright future, choose something that is demanding, such as mechanical or civil engineering." Listening to this advice was probably the worst mistake that I have made in my life up to now. So, for a while I put my computers away and took an interest in cars; I spent some years racing, and building and tuning cars. Later in life, I started to study business and marketing. After obtaining two masters degrees in business studies, I still was only able to get a job related to my engineering experience. I then started to think about doing a PhD. My hope was to do research on renewable energy. But it did not happen. I started building PCs again, inspired by one of my friends. I built a PC with an Intel i7 2600k processor[3] just when the new 3rd generation Intel processor was about to come to the market. When I moved to Europe, I continued working with computers, pursuing my lost passion. And then, as described above, I got involved in the GPU mining world.

→ Help me to improve the book

I have written this book using Microsoft Word. I know the text may not be as complete as some reader would like. Also, as said earlier, I am not a computer software expert, so I have not gone beyond what has been quoted on the web and in other references. <u>So, if you have any suggestions on how I might improve these guidelines, I would be only too happy to receive them and take them into account in any future revision.</u> If you find this book helpful or you are interested in helping me make a better content, please don't hesitate to contact me. I would also like to hear

---

[3] A processor or CPU is a central processing unit. It is an electronic chip and component that does most of computational work of a computer; it is the brain of any computer. Read more about it in Chapter 2.

your opinions—all of your comments and criticisms would be welcomed, so please send them to me by email: ermiya.karan@gpumining.space

→ Legal disclaimer

This book presents the writer's personal recommendations based on his research and experience in building a GPU mining rig and trading cryptocurrency. Trading and investing in such currencies is risky and readers are advised to do their own research before building a GPU mining rig, or making any trading or investment decisions.

While the author has made every effort to ensure that the information and instructions contained in this book are accurate, the author disclaims all responsibility for any errors or omissions, including, without limitation, responsibility for damages resulting from the use of or reliance on this work. Use of the information and instructions contained in this book is at the reader's own risk. If any code samples or other technology this work contains or describes is subject to open source licenses or the intellectual property rights of others, it is the reader's responsibility to ensure that his or her use thereof complies with such licenses and/or rights.

Many of the designations used by manufacturers and sellers to distinguish their products are claimed as trademarks. Where those designations appear in this book, and the author was aware of a trademark claim, the designations have been printed in capital letters or with an initial capital letter.

Acknowledgments

My first language and the language in which I was schooled is Farsi (Persian). I only started learning English when I was 12 years old. This was in the Paran Language Institute in Tehran. I developed my technical writing skills in different academic topics when I was studying for a Master of International Business at the University of Wollongong (Australia) and later, when I was studying for a Master of Mechanical Engineering at Rochester Institute of Technology (USA). However, I was aware that I made many mistakes in writing of this book and I needed someone to review it from an editorial point of view. I was extremely fortunate that **Dr. Anthony Wrixon** offered me to do this for me. His acceptation was the best thing that has happened to me in many years. So, 2017 started spectacularly for me! I am deeply grateful for all the help and effort that he has put into this book. It would have been impossible for me to have written this book correctly without his technical writing skills and outstanding observations. I wish him and his lovely wife, Nicole, healthy and prosperous lives.

This book represents the efforts and contributions of many people who have helped me indirectly. I have taken so much information from the internet and publicly available websites. In particular, this book has been written with the help of the Ethereum and GPU mining community. My work on this book was encouraged and supported by my family. I am deeply thankful.

Chapter 1

What is GPU mining? A short review of cryptocurrency and GPU mining platforms.

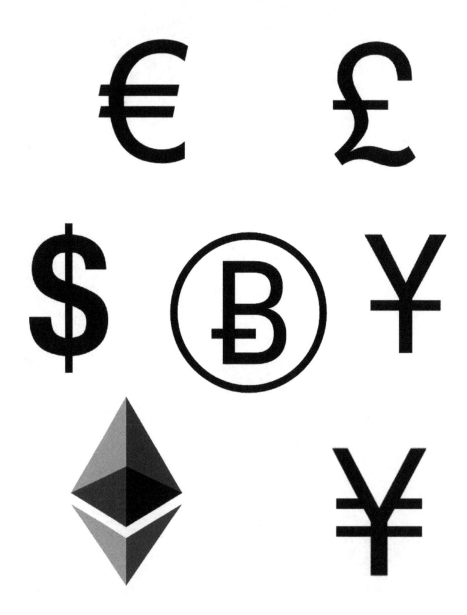

1.1.Currency in general

A currency refers to money in any form when in actual use or circulation as a medium of exchange, especially circulating banknotes and coins. A more general definition is a system of money (monetary units) in common use, especially in a nation. Under this definition, U.S. Dollars, British Pounds, Australian Dollars, and European Euros are examples of currency [1]. We also have <u>fiat money</u> and commodity money. Fiat money is a currency established as money by government regulation or law. It differs from commodity money and representative money. Commodity money is created from a good, often a precious metal such as gold or silver, which has uses other than as a medium of exchange (such a good is called a commodity), while representative money simply represents a claim on such a good [2]. In the past, the money which was produced by a state was considered as representative money because the printed money was backed by gold or silver and for each amount of printed money, some amount of precious metal was held as a reserve to maintain the value of the money. However, the link between the U.S. Dollar and gold was abolished in 1971.

Fiat money is printed by the Central Bank of the particular nation or system and most of the time it is backed by precious metals such as gold or silver. There is no outer disciplinary organization that says how much of what currency is to be made and distributed. This is based on the government's decision and balancing of demand and supply. When too much money is being printed, and enters the market, high inflation rates and devaluation of that currency often occurs. However, the U.S. BEP[1] states that "90% of printed U.S. Dollar money is just a replacement of old and damaged" [3]. Accordingly, during the fiscal year 2014, the Bureau of Engraving and Printing delivered approximately 6.6 billion notes to the Federal Reserve (approximately 24.8 million notes a day) with a face value of approximately $560 million [4], and in the fiscal year 2016, the BEP delivered 7.6 billion notes to the Federal Reserve.

Number in bracket stands for the reference at the end of each chapter, the hyperlink in blue connects to the web page of the source.

Travel and tourism are the main driving forces for having foreign currency; trade and business purposes come second. A currency can be exchanged for another, and the exchange rate and the exchange ratio depends on many economic and financial factors. A local currency exchanger of a country usually trades best its national currency with other major currencies, according to BIS[2]. In 2016, the most traded currencies by value

---

[1] BEP is U.S. Bureau of Engraving and Printing.
[2] BIS is Bank for International Settlements

were: USD with 87.6%, EUR with 31.4%, JPY with 21.6%, GBP with 12.8%, AUD with 6.9%, CAD with 5.1%, CHF with 4.8% and CNY with 4.0% [5].

1.2. Cryptocurrency

A cryptocurrency has major differences with a regular currency in terms of:

1.2.1. Shape and form: cryptocurrency is a digital money while a fiat money is physical, and can be produced in the form of notes or coins. A regular currency can exist only on digital records, for instance, you have $100 in bank, but the bank may not actually have your $100 stored in a safe; it may have spent it on things like investments or loans. If you demand your $100, it may require some time to deliver it to you, so your actual money only existed on records, in digital terms, in your bank account. A cryptocurrency does not have a physical representation, it only exists on ledgers and records, in computers and servers, but you may exchange it with another currency like Dollars or Euros.

1.2.2. Operations: cryptocurrency is founded on peer-to-peer (P2P) networks system. In a P2P[3] system which is based on a file sharing system, every computer, miner (a miner consists of a mining device, or a mining computer that generates cryptocurrency. Read more about mining devices and miners later in this chapter) or person is a node of the entire network, and everybody who is connected is both a consumer and a supplier at the same time [6]. **The backbone and the main difference between a cryptocurrency and a fiat currency is how it operates through its network.** Without a network of computers, without a P2P system, cryptocurrency does not work. Moreover, most of the advantages of cryptocurrency come from its P2P network system. Being decentralized, it is empowered by the P2P network capabilities. How does it work? The heart of a cryptocurrency is based on its blockchain; this is a large set of data that represents every transaction. All purchases are recorded in the blockchain, confirming an owner's possession of the particular cryptocurrency. When you download an Ether or Bitcoin wallet, you are downloading the blockchain, so every user has a copy of the entire network[4] [7]. As Blockgeeks.com says, a cryptocurrency, like Bitcoin, consists of a network of peers. Every peer has a record of the complete history of all

Text with green highlight is important to read.

---

[3] I'm not intending to explain all about P2P networking here. Presumably you have some idea, but it is always better to read more about it online. Understanding the P2P networking system is the first step to understand the whole cryptocurrency idea.

[4] Taken from article of Katherine Sagona-Stophel, Government Analyst, Thomson Reuters.

transactions and thus of the balance of every account. A transaction is a file that says, "Bob gives X Bitcoin to Alice" and is signed by Bob. After signing, a transaction is broadcast on the network, sent from one peer to every other peer. This is basic P2P-technology. The transaction is known almost immediately by the whole network. But only after a specific amount of time is it confirmed.

Blockgeeks.com continues by explaining that **confirmation** is a critical concept in cryptocurrencies. You could, in fact, say that cryptocurrencies are all about confirmation. As long as a transaction is unconfirmed, it is pending and can be forged. When a transaction is confirmed, it is set in stone. It is no longer forgeable, and it can't be reversed as it is part of an immutable record of historical transactions of the blockchain. Only miners can confirm transactions. This is their job in a cryptocurrency network. They take transactions, stamp them as legitimate and spread them in the network. After a transaction is confirmed by a miner, every node has to add it to its database. It has become part of the blockchain.

1.2.3. **Governing body**: the operation of a cryptocurrency is different from that of a centralized banking system, like the Federal Reserve system, where governments control the value of their currencies like USD through the process of printing fiat money. Governments have no control over cryptocurrencies as they operate totally independently A cryptocurrency is produced by the entire cryptocurrency system collectively (the entire system consists of all of the mining system and the mining rigs of the entire network), at a rate which is defined when the system is created and which is publicly announced. So, an established cryptocurrency, such as Bitcoin or Ether, has a big community which includes founders, investors, programmers, enthusiasts, miners, etc. that are responsible for making and generating the cryptocurrency; they are not employed by a specific company or bank and their citizenship is unknown.

1.3.Cryptocurrency characteristics

Not being governed by an organization doesn't mean it runs by itself. There are many rules and regulations that any cryptocurrency operates under. There are major differences between each cryptocurrency. These differences can be categorized as follows:

1.3.1. Identity of cryptocurrency: a cryptocurrency can only be created if miners solve a cryptographic puzzle. This puzzle is also called a 'proof of work' system. According to Bitcoinwiki, "A proof of work is a piece of data which is difficult (costly, time-consuming) to produce but easy for others to verify and which satisfies certain requirements. Producing a proof of work can be a random process with low probability so that a lot of trial and error is required on average before a valid proof of work is generated." The difficulty in solving this puzzle increases with the amount of computational power that the whole of the miner community brings, and there is a limit to the amount of the particular cryptocurrency that can be created in a given amount of time. This is part of the agreement that no peer in the network can break. Each cryptocurrency works with a cryptographic hash function, and every cryptocurrency has a puzzle program, to which a miner of that cryptocurrency must find the answer. In other words, the mining computers are required to search for the right meaningless string such that the block satisfies a certain arbitrary condition. Specifically, the hash of the block has to satisfy a certain number of leading zeros. What are hashes? **Hashes** are one-way functions, so there is no easy way to find the right **nonce**[5] or otherwise to correctly engineer a block. The only known way to find a good nonce is simply to try randomly until one turns out to work.

Moreover, a hash algorithm turns an arbitrarily large amount of data into a fixed-length hash. The same hash will always result from the same data, but modifying the data by even one bit will completely change the hash. Like all computer data, hashes are large numbers, and are usually written in hexadecimal form. BitCoin uses the **SHA-256** hash algorithm to generate verifiably "random" numbers in a way that requires a predictable amount of CPU effort. [8]

For example, SHA-1 is a cryptographic hash function. The result of the function is usually expressed as a 160-bit hex number. SHA-1 was developed by the NSA. SHA-1 is widely considered the successor to MD5 (visit the link here to make your own SHA-1 hash).

---

[5] As Wikipedia explains: "In cryptography, a nonce is an arbitrary number that may only be used once. It is similar in spirit to a nonce word, hence the name. It is often a random or pseudo-random number issued in an authentication protocol to ensure that old communications cannot be reused in replay attacks. They can also be useful as initialization vectors and in cryptographic hash function."

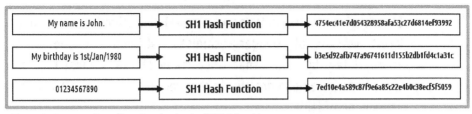

Figure 1 - Presentation of input and output of SHA1 function

SHA-256 of Bitcoin generates a 256-bit hex number. Due to the security vulnerability of SHA-1, it is being retired for most government uses. SHA-2 is similar to SHA-256 and has been used since 2010. SHA-2 includes significant changes from its predecessor, SHA-1. The SHA-2 family consists of six hash functions with digests (hash values) that are 224, 256, 384 or 512 bits: SHA-224, SHA-256, SHA-384, SHA-512, SHA-512/224, SHA-512/256. Most of applications are now transiting to SHA-3 which is a 512-bit hex [9].

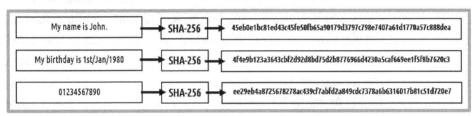

Figure 2 – Presentation of SHA-256 function and its output in 256-bit (32-byte) hash value.

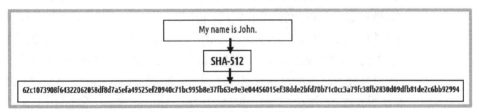

Figure 3 – Example of a random input and Sha-512 hash algorithm output.

So, in summary, the hash algorithm is a one-way function. There is no way of guessing the input from the output; the only way is to try different inputs into the hash function and compare the results. Imagine Bitcoin network says the output of hash algorithm is:

"55e15b6c11480345d913bdca7234b78359667a1559eb956b703e25488645190a"

A computer must go through billions of random inputs to generate such an output. An **ASIC-miner S9** which is a special Bitcoin mining computer can do ~14 terahashes per second!! This can be purchased for about $1500 and consumes about 1400 watts of electricity.

Ethash is the planned PoW (proof of work) algorithm for Ethereum 1.0. It is the latest version of Dagger-Hashimoto, although it should no longer appropriately be called that since many of the original features of both algorithms have been drastically changed in the last months of research and development[6] [10].

According to bitcoingmining.com "During the winter of 2011, a new industry sprang up with custom equipment that pushed the performance standards of the algorithm even higher. The first wave of these specialty bitcoin mining devices were easy-to-use Bitcoin miners based on field-programmable gate-array (FPGA) processors and attached to computers using a convenient USB connection. FPGA miners used much less power than CPU's or GPU's and made concentrated mining farms possible for the first time [11]. Application-specific integrated-circuit chips (**ASICs**) are bitcoin mining hardware created solely to solve Bitcoin blocks. They have only minimal requirements for other normal computer applications. Consequently, ASIC Bitcoin-mining systems can solve Bitcoin blocks much quicker and use less electricity or power than older bitcoin-mining hardware like CPUs, GPUs or FPGAs. As Bitcoin mining increases in popularity and the Bitcoin price rises so does the value of ASIC Bitcoin-mining hardware. As more Bitcoin-mining hardware is deployed and more miners share resources to solve the problem, the security of the Bitcoin network becomes increasingly more difficult. Diving deeper, the difficulty level of mining operations with Bitcoin tends to adjust itself after every 2016 blocks. The difficulty of the adjustment will depend on the network's performance, which takes into account the availability of the hashing power and the average time taken to discover new blocks. If the block generation time is faster than 6 new blocks an hour, then the difficulty will increase. Similarly, if the block discovery time is higher than 10 minutes, owing to increased difficulty, the time will be reduced to ensure a constant rate of generation.

Also, this makes it impossible to profitably compete without a Bitcoin ASIC system. Furthermore, Bitcoin ASIC technology keeps getting faster, more efficient and more productive, so it keeps pushing the limits of what makes the best Bitcoin mining hardware. At the moment, the new S9 Antminer can do 11 TH/s, with only 1078 watts at a price of ~$1300. By comparison, a 6-GPU mining

---

[6] Read more about Ethash in "Analysis of Ethash, Ethereum's Proof-of-Work puzzle" article, link is here!

rig with six of AMD RX 470 4GB, consumes 1000 watts and at a cost of ~$2000, makes only 2 GH/s * 6 = 12 GH/s, almost 1000 times less.

On the negative side, ASIC miners are not cheap, not everyone can build them (they have complex circuitry and cannot be assembled or made like an ordinary computer). But as a miner (someone who operates in a mining business or has a mining system), you can buy them and let them run. Also, these days, the profit generation is not too high. During 2014, the next generation (not Bitcoin based) of cryptocurrencies started in which developers tried to code the currency toward **ASIC-resistance programming**. For example, the Ethereum platform is totally GPU friendly, and the algorithm does not favor any machines other than simple desktop GPUs for mining. In GPU mining, the concept is "fair-mining" which means that everyone can build and access the mining equipment and engage with the platform. In addition, in the past, we learnt that most BitCoin miners became obsolete soon after the next more efficient ASIC miners entered. These made them unprofitable even to run, and the cost of the investment was never recovered. On the other hand, **Ethash** proof of work is ASIC resistant and **memory hard**; it requires a 2+ GB of memory to run the algorithm and it is GPU friendly by design [12].

To make a long story short, it can be said that each cryptocurrency has its own puzzles to be solved and the miner get rewards by finding the solution.

1.3.2. Currency production and rewarding system: Here is the one main difference between cryptocurrencies and fiat currencies. In a fully decentralized monetary system, there is no central authority that regulates the monetary base. Instead, currency is created by the nodes of a peer-to-peer network. The cryptocurrency generation algorithm defines, in advance, how the currency will be created and at what rate [13].

Accordingly, by a default of programming, the total number of bitcoins has an asymptote (i.e., approaches to finite number) of 21 million Bitcoins. The last Bitcoin will be mined in 2140. The successful miner finding the new block is rewarded with newly created bitcoins and transaction fees. As of 9 July 2016, the reward amounted to 12.5 newly created bitcoins per block added to the blockchain. To claim the reward, a special transaction called a coinbase is included with the processed payments. All bitcoins in existence have been created in such coinbase transactions. The bitcoin protocol specifies that the reward for adding a block will be halved after every 210,000 blocks (approximately every four years). Eventually, the reward will decrease to zero as the number of bitcoins approach the limit of 21 million bitcoins. This limit was set artificially by bitcoin's inventor, Nakamoto, at bitcoin's inception [14][7].

With the Ethereum platform, it is a different story, as ethereum.org states "according to the terms agreed by all parties on the 2014 presale, issuance of ether is capped at 18 million ethers per year (this number equals 25% of the initial supply). This means that while the absolute issuance is fixed, the relative inflation is decreased every year." In theory, if this issuance were kept indefinitely, then at some point the rate of new tokens created every year would reach the average amount lost yearly (by misuse, accidental key lost, death of holders, etc.) and an equilibrium would be reached. Five ethers are created in every block (roughly every 15–17 seconds) to the miner of the block, and 2–3 ethers are sometimes sent to another miner, if they were also able to find a solution but his/her block wasn't included (called uncle/aunt) [15].

1.4. Engaging with Cryptocurrency and Mining process

So how can a person or an organization be engaged with the cryptocurrency? Here I summarize difference scenarios that might arise.

1.4.1. Trade in exchange market

Being a kind of currency makes cryptocurrency a commodity that can be traded or exchanged with other fiat currencies or cryptocurrencies. At the moment, few cryptocurrencies such as Bitcoin, Ethereum, etc. can be cashed or exchanged with real fiat money, and many of the non-popular cryptocurrencies can only be exchanged with other cryptocurrencies. Also, cryptocurrency is not yet accepted by the normal banking systems, although there is a momentum toward adding Bitcoin to the exchange basket of some banking systems, other cryptocurrencies have a long way to go before they can enter the life of ordinary people. In spite of the uncertainty related to how banking systems and money investment firms will respond toward cryptocurrencies, tens of cryptocurrency exchange platforms already exist that let a user to trade them efficiently.

How big is this trade market? You are not going to believe it. At the end of January 2017, the Bitcoin market capitalization is $14,894,755,171 ($14.8 billion!) and during the last 24 hours, $91,746,600 at a price of ~$923 have been traded. The Ethereum

---

[7] There are hundreds of articles to read and study online on how Bitcoin algorithm works and how the miner is being rewarded. The focus of this book is on GPU mining, concentrating on the hardware and the mining rig.

market cap is $949,411,663, and during the same 24 hours, $7,923,710 of ETH at a price of $10.77 have been traded [16]. Statistics and information of the market capitalization and trade volume is available from most of the cryptocurrency trade websites, such as coinmarketcap.com, and also in most of the websites of mining pools. About 644 currencies are currently being traded online.

Let's talk about the big traders in today's cryptocurrency market. When you study the statistical data on a cryptocurrency exchange, you will find out who has the biggest trade volume in the market. According to coinmarketcap.com, **Poloniex** has the most trade with ~ $2.4 million on 5th Feb. 2017. **Poloniex** was founded in January 2014, is based in the United States, and is a leading cryptocurrency exchange offering over 100 Bitcoin (BTC) markets for trading [17]. **Kraken** was founded in 2011. It is San Francisco-based and is the largest Bitcoin exchange in Euro volume and liquidity and it also trades Canadian Dollars, U.S. Dollars, British pounds and Japanese yen. Kraken was the first Bitcoin exchange to have its trading price and volume displayed on the Bloomberg Terminal [18]. Based in Hong Kong and founded in 2012, **Bitfinex** was the largest bitcoin exchange by U.S. Dollar volume prior to being hacked. Bitfinex had lots of troubles inside its platform and with the outside world. On August 2016, it was hacked and almost $60m worth Bitcoin were stolen. As a result, the price of Bitcoin fell by 20% [19].

Table 1 - The top 20 traders of Ethereum in exchange market on 22. May.2017. Ethereum is the world's 2nd largest cryptocurrency which is being traded after Bitcoin.

#	Source	Pair	Volume (24h)	Price	Volume (%)
1	Poloniex	ETH/BTC	$289,462,000	$169.77	24.51%
2	Bithumb	ETH/KRW	$170,825,000	$222.12	14.47%
3	Coinone	ETH/KRW	$117,878,000	$221.05	9.98%
4	GDAX	ETH/USD	$91,443,800	$172.01	7.74%
5	Korbit	ETH/KRW	$66,280,800	$222.75	5.61%
6	Bitfinex	ETH/USD	$65,145,500	$166.00	5.52%
7	Kraken	ETH/EUR	$57,888,200	$163.36	4.90%
8	Kraken	ETH/BTC	$50,193,100	$169.22	4.25%
9	Yunbi	ETH/CNY	$31,845,100	$184.33	2.70%
10	Bitfinex	ETH/BTC	$30,905,500	$168.80	2.62%
11	Bittrex	ETH/BTC	$26,211,700	$169.59	2.22%
12	Kraken	ETH/USD	$25,295,800	$164.00	2.14%
13	BTC-E	ETH/USD	$16,394,100	$167.40	1.39%
14	Gemini	ETH/USD	$14,980,700	$167.63	1.27%
15	Livecoin	ETH/BTC	$13,136,800	$164.45	1.11%
16	BTC-E	ETH/BTC	$13,107,000	$168.66	1.11%
17	Poloniex	ETH/USDT	$12,922,500	$164.81	1.09%
18	GDAX	ETH/BTC	$12,569,600	$168.93	1.06%
19	Gemini	ETH/BTC	$7,237,220	$167.62	0.61%
20	bitFlyer	ETH/BTC	$4,552,770	$175.68	0.39%

Ethereum Classic (ETC) market is much smaller, but it is still the 7th most traded cryptocurrency in the world.

Table 2 – Top traders of Ethereum Classic by volume on 22 May 2017.

#	Source	Pair	Volume (24h)	Price	Volume (%)
1	Bithumb	ETC/KRW	$42,298,100	$11.29	23.39%
2	Poloniex	ETC/BTC	$30,824,700	$8.70	17.04%
3	Korbit	ETC/KRW	$21,927,300	$11.19	12.12%
4	Coinone	ETC/KRW	$21,589,900	$11.25	11.94%
5	Bitfinex	ETC/USD	$15,030,200	$8.56	8.31%
6	Yunbi	ETC/CNY	$9,387,860	$9.57	5.19%
7	Bitfinex	ETC/BTC	$7,237,510	$8.71	4.00%
8	Bittrex	ETC/BTC	$7,014,140	$8.75	3.88%
9	Kraken	ETC/BTC	$6,439,250	$8.64	3.56%
10	Poloniex	ETC/USDT	$3,934,900	$8.35	2.18%
11	Kraken	ETC/EUR	$3,374,340	$8.30	1.87%
12	Poloniex	ETC/ETH	$3,047,880	$8.70	1.69%
13	Yuanbao	ETC/CNY	$2,939,450	$9.93	1.63%
14	Kraken	ETC/ETH	$2,467,890	$8.83	1.36%
15	Kraken	ETC/USD	$1,770,430	$8.48	0.98%
16	BTER	ETC/CNY	$1,250,690	$9.49	0.69%
17	BTC Markets	ETC/AUD	$76,091	$8.03	0.04%
18	USD X	ETC/USD	$71,004	$9.78	0.04%
19	Bittrex	ETC/ETH	$51,723	$9.14	0.03%
20	Gatehub	XRP/ETC	$28,652	$8.52	0.02%

Not all cryptocurrencies in existence can be mined, Ripple(XPR) is one of them. According to Merkle Blog "The Ripple network works in a rather different manner compared to Bitcoin or even Ethereum. Positioning itself as the global settlement network, Ripple is not your average cryptocurrency by any means. Obtaining Ripple can only be done by buying the currency from various exchanges, as there is no option to generate XRP by mining. A total of 100 billion XRP has been created once the project launched. A few coins are destroyed every time a transaction takes place" [20]. Table below shows the market capitalization of Ripple at end of May 2017.

#	Exchange	Pair	Price	volume (BTC)	Volume
1	Poloniex	XRP/BTC	0.00010170 BTC	55338.478	68%
2	Kraken	XRP/BTC	0.00010087 BTC	7739.67	9%
3	Bittrex	XRP/BTC	0.00010294 BTC	6833.409	8%
4	Poloniex	XRP/USDT	0.2599 USDT	3685.844	4%
5	Kraken	XRP/EUR	0.2405 EUR	2446.866	3%
6	Kraken	XRP/USD	0.2600 USD	1506.636	1%
7	Bitfinex	XRP/BTC	0.00010224 BTC	1151.686	1%
8	Jubi	XRP/CNY	2.1300 CNY	873.492	1%
9	Bitfinex	XRP/USD	0.2624 USD	838.915	1%
10	Anxpro	XRP/BTC	0.00010798 BTC	65.323	0%
11	Kraken	XRP/CAD	0.3489 CAD	33.009	0%

Table 3 is similar to Table 1. The data have been taken from worldcoinindex.com. The main difference in this table is that **CHBTC** is on the top of the traders. Founded in 2013, CHBTC is one of the mainstream digital currency exchanges in China.

Table 3 - Top 25 Ethereum traders of the world by trade volume including CHBTC.
Source is https://www.worldcoinindex.com/coin/ethereum

#	Exchange	Pair	last price	volume
1	Poloniex	ETH/BTC	$ 167.915136	$ 282,326,436
2	Bithumb	ETH/KRW	$ 172.179590	$ 127,626,857
3	GDAX	ETH/USD	$ 174.573599	$ 95,042,664
4	Bitfinex	ETH/USD	$ 169.562903	$ 66,601,119
5	CHBTC	ETH/CNY	$ 196.465474	$ 53,142,605
6	Kraken	ETH/BTC	$ 167.939626	$ 50,745,380
7	Korbit	ETH/KRW	$ 171.151101	$ 48,881,745
8	Bitfinex	ETH/BTC	$ 167.937402	$ 31,077,309
9	Yunbi	ETH/CNY	$ 176.450405	$ 29,687,968
10	Bittrex	ETH/BTC	$ 168.239000	$ 25,828,732
11	BTC-e	ETH/USD	$ 168.709380	$ 16,315,245
12	Gemini	ETH/USD	$ 167.637161	$ 16,368,214
13	Livecoin	ETH/BTC	$ 167.937402	$ 13,811,826
14	GDAX	ETH/BTC	$ 172.986646	$ 13,293,127
15	BTC-e	ETH/BTC	$ 167.270101	$ 13,095,135
16	Gemini	ETH/BTC	$ 170.717823	$ 7,859,640
17	Yobit	ETH/BTC	$ 169.294247	$ 4,161,700
18	Quoine	ETH/JPY	$ 136.564182	$ 3,144,446
19	Bter	ETH/CNY	$ 175.706275	$ 2,033,391

1.4.2. Making cryptocurrency and running a mining system

Unlike fiat money, like the Euro or Dollar, you can make your own cryptocurrency; you can mine coins at home whereas you cannot print money or go and mine gold or silver. However, by design, in any cryptocurrency which is based on peer-2-peer networking, each node is a member of the whole community and can be engaged in generating the cryptocurrency. How **difficult** it is? Not very difficult really! This book is written to guide someone who wishes to build a GPU mining rig. Any person with some knowledge of using a computer and with a little study can make a mining computer. How much does it **cost**? Later in Chapter 5 you can read all about it, but a simple mining computer can be built for only about $100 for experimental purposes, although it may not be very profitable.

Thousands of people are engaged in the generation of cryptocurrencies and mining. For instance, on dwarfpool.com [21], an **Ethereum** mining pool[8], in 5th Feb. 2017, there were 13,592 active workers, with a total mining power of 1,499,061 MH/s (mega hashes per second). If you divide the mining power by the number of active workers, that makes a mining power of ~110 MH/s per worker. As said earlier, the computational power of any mining rig is measured by how many hash functions it can run per second. Hashing power of any particular mining system is different on each mining platform. For instance, a mining rig that is able to hash 100 MH/s on Ethereum may make only 40 MH/s on the **Dash** platform. To make 110 MH/s, you would require an Ethereum mining computer that has a minimum of five GPUs[9], and each of these GPU mining rigs would cost on average $2000. As of that date, Dwarfpool had only ~17% [22] of the share of the whole Ethereum mining workers, which implies that there were ~84,000 active workers online. The network hash-rate power was 8,085 GH/s. So, put simply, the average active mining power of a worker was 8,085G/84,000, which is 96.5 MH/s. Considering the average cost of a system with 96.5 MH/s is about ~$1500 ($1500 is my estimation of cost. I give more information on the cost of a mining rig in Chapter 5!), the total cost of the whole mining system would be 84,000 x $1500 = $126m; this would have been the total amount that had been invested to generate and mine Ethereum at that time.

---

[8] A mining pool is where so many workers and miners work together to solve the block puzzle and later on take a share of value., Read more about it at the end of Chapter 5.
[9] More about GPU mining hardware in Chapter 2 and onwards. For now, just read it and pass.

1.4.3. Use cryptocurrency in real life?! Be a consumer!

As said earlier, a cryptocurrency has many advantages over a typical printable fiat money. At the moment, many stores, companies, websites and organizations accept payments directly in Bitcoin. However, this facility is not yet available for the second largest cryptocurrency, Ethereum. Bitcoin market capitalizations are currently ~$15 billion which is almost 15 times bigger than Ether of Ethereum (there is another variation of the Ethereum project called Ether Classic, Ether Classic of Ethereum platform). Ether is still a relatively young platform and under development and therefore vulnerable to market uncertainties. It probably has another few years before it can be regarded as mature. So, as of now, at the beginning of 2017, we have only the mighty Bitcoin that can be spent to buy products and services. Even so, using Bitcoin is like running uphill at the moment; it's so much easier to buy and own Bitcoin than to spend it, although almost all of the cryptocurrency brokers will cash Bitcoin immediately. You can read more on how to buy Bitcoin on the webpage of "Buying Bitcoins (the newbie version)" on the Bitcoinwiki [23].

You can travel with Bitcoin and buy air tickets; many travel and tourism websites such as Expedia.com [24] and Cheapair.com [25] accept Bitcoin. However, obtaining a refund following cancellation is a little more complicated or may not be possible. However, at the moment, there are only a few airlines that accept Bitcoin directly, such as airBaltic.com [26]. Airlines policies on accepting Bitcoin are therefore not currently consistent. Similar inconsistencies in the market toward Bitcoin existed and are mostly influenced by the position of the banking sector.

A shop or store that accepts direct Bitcoin payment usually exhibits the above sign on the door. You can add money to your Microsoft [27] account by Bitcoin and spend it on applications, software, products or games.

The newegg.com [28], the giant online electronics retailer, also accepts Bitcoin.

The biggest online game retailer, Steam, also accepts Bitcoin.

And the list continues. On the website 99bitcoins.com [29], there are many comprehensive lists of companies that accept Bitcoin payments. However, you will need to double check the availability of the service, as many of the payment facilities are done through financial brokers, such as Coinbase and many of them may no longer be valid.

Although you can spend your Bitcoin easily on the web, in everyday life you may have lots of troubles. If you go a little far from the central hubs and major cities, you will find that there are no shops that accept Bitcoin. Even in a big city, it may seem that you have a foreign currency. Imagine you have Euros in the USA or Dollars in Europe, not everyone will accept your foreign currency. So, what are your options? Imagine you have 10 Bitcoins units, which are valued at around $9,000 and you want to spend your money on something. You will need first to go online, exchange your Bitcoin to a currency that is linked to your bank account, wait a few hours or days for completion of the process. So, Bitcoin plays as a middleman here not as a direct bartering tool as is the case with fiat money. Ethereum acts in the same way.

Let's not get ahead of ourselves, after all you heard, would you like to know how many registered wallet addresses there are at the moment? There were in fact only 11.8 million users as of 9th Feb. 2017 [30], 13.251 million users on 22th April 2017 and the average growth rate was 22k–25k every day.

The actual growth rate is given by a fifth-degree polynomial equation:

$$y = (2E - 6)x^5 - (0.4619)x^4 + (39491)x^3 - (2E19)x^2 + (4E13)x - (3E17)$$

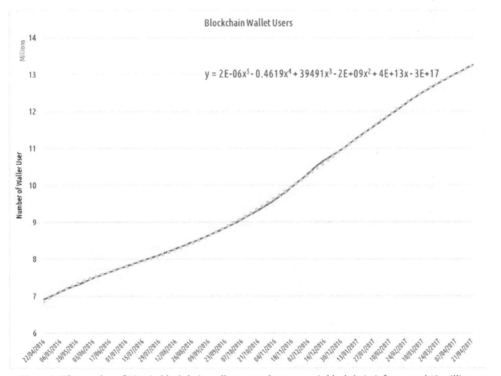

Figure 4 - The number of Bitcoin blockchain wallet users, data source is blockchain.info, around 12 million users at beginning of 2017.

Based on the current growth rate, the numbers of addresses will grow by another 9 million by the end of 2017. Many of these newly created addresses belong to existing users who are considered as recurring users, while not each wallet address binds to one person and anyone has the liberty of making an unlimited number of addresses. As a result, the actual number of Bitcoin users is relatively small. With the Ethereum network, the situation is even less promising; most of the activities either bind to Bitcoin and follow its path or only play as a medium valued cryptocurrency that can be traded with fiat money through exchange brokers. There are no shops or businesses that accept Ether directly, nor are you able to buy things online. So, if you have some Ether, you have to first cash them with a broker and then exchange them for Bitcoins or fiat currency that your local bank will accept. There is an informative article with the title of "Use Cases of Ethereum In Different Sectors 2016" [31], which refers to many potential uses of Ethereum in today's real world.

1.5.Dark side of cryptocurrency

The main problem with cryptocurrencies at the moment is their age; they are simply not mature. The eldest one, Bitcoin, was born around 2008. The technology on which cryptocurrency is based is P2P networking, which is less than 20 years old. Almost all cryptocurrencies are in the early development stage. Nevertheless, I believe that the future belongs to digital currency and we are just at the beginning of the journey. There are no solid studies yet about the impact of using digital currency at the national scale, how to evolve the economy when the banking system is decentralized and everyone is able to print their own money. As said earlier, the existence and the value of Bitcoin are linked to other currencies, a matter that is facilitated by brokers and cryptocurrency exchangers. As a result, restriction on the operation of financial institutions with Bitcoin would hurt its value.

The biggest economic problem with any cryptocurrency is the central banking system. Central banks do not agree with the fundamentals, rules and regulations of cryptocurrency. Many banks are hostile toward the Bitcoin users and accounts that are linked to a Bitcoin wallet or cryptocurrency [32]. There is however a list of **Bitcoin-friendly banks** which can be found on the Bitcoin forum and users of Bitcoin tend to report on incidents of freezing, closure and termination [33]. Also, in the international banking system, AML/KYC plays a major role. Anti-money laundering (AML) is a term mainly used in the financial and legal industries to describe the legal controls that require financial institutions and other regulated entities to prevent, detect, and report money laundering [34]. The main reason that banks oppose cryptocurrency activities is because of **AML/KYC Requirements**. Know your customer (KYC) is the process of a business identifying and verifying the identity of its clients. The term is also used to refer to the bank regulation that governs these activities [35]. In some countries, like Australia, a new system of customer due diligence (CDD) is in place. CDD is central to an effective anti-money laundering and counter-terrorism financing (AML/CTF) regime [36]. While banks see cryptocurrency as a competitor that tries to bypass many established money regulations, it is also extremely risky and costly for banks to have bitcoin businesses on their books at the moment [37]. Also, the problems for bitcoin begin with its legal status as 'money' or otherwise. According to hg.org "In the United States, businesses that transmit money, such as PayPal, Western Union, and MoneyGram, must comply with the regulations adopted by the U.S. Treasury Department [38]. The Treasury Department's Financial Crimes Enforcement Network (FinCEN[10]) and anti-money-

---

[10] From FinCEN.org website "The mission of the Financial Crimes Enforcement Network is to safeguard the financial system from illicit use and combat money laundering and promote national security through the collection, analysis, and dissemination of financial intelligence and strategic use of financial authorities."

laundering unit are concerned that Bitcoin is operating outside of these regulations, even though it is effectively carrying on the same type of business, just using Bitcoins instead of a nationally recognized fiat currency. For over a decade, the Treasury Department has required money transmitters to register with FinCEN, enact controls to prevent money laundering, report suspicious financial activity, and obtain state licenses." [39]

Being decentralized and easy to transfer and trade, Bitcoin is attractive to those who wish to undertake gray operations. Imagine the assets of an entity are frozen because of fraud in a country and most of the money and capitals are in Bitcoin in a wallet address, the Bitcoin can nevertheless be transferred within few minutes to an unknown address in an unknown country. Why? Because there is no governing body to stop the transaction. Bitcoin is decentralized and independent and nobody can override the transaction process. Even if you know where the transferred wallet and Bitcoin are located, how can you pursue the Bitcoin money in another wallet? It is extremely difficult if not impossible because: 1. The wallet addresses are not bonded to a single entity; 2. the judicial system of the first country has no jurisdiction rights over the second country; and 3. the Bitcoin that exist in a wallet can be cashed by many exchange brokers online and be transferred to another bank account. There are no international guidelines, rules and regulations on how judicial systems might work in such circumstances. Many years ago, people might care about how fast a car could drive, without paying much attention on how safe it was. Today safety comes first. The situation is similar with Bitcoin. It is fast, and efficient, but is it safe for the user? How can Bitcoin be made to comply with national policies and financial requirements? I believe that there is a low probability that a cryptocurrency with the current functioning platform, could bypass the many barriers that organizations such as FinCEN have created, and be accepted by a regular baking system. At the moment two major issues with cryptocurrencies must be dealt with; first, the difficulty of tracking the source and destination of funds and transactions and second, the anonymity of the owner. Bitcoin, Ethereum and other cryptocurrency developers must establish a code of practice that is consistent with the regulatory requirements of the banking system, while preserving the good features of their cryptocurrency.

References

[1]   Wikipedia, the free encyclopedia, 2017, "Currency," Wikipedia.
[2]   Wikipedia, the free encyclopedia, 2017, "Fiat Money," Wikipedia.
[3]   Bureau of Engraving and Printing, "U.S. Currency" [Online]. Available:
        http://www.moneyfactory.gov/uscurrency.html. [Accessed: 13-Jan-2017].
[4]   U.S. Department of the Treasury, "Production & Circulation" [Online]. Available:
        https://www.treasury.gov/resource-
        center/faqs/Currency/Pages/edu_faq_currency_production.aspx. [Accessed: 13-Jan-2017].
[5]   Bank for International Settlements, "Triennial Central Bank Survey" [Online]. Available:
        http://www.bis.org/publ/rpfx16fx.pdf. [Accessed: 23-Feb-2017].
[6]   Wikipedia, the free encyclopedia, 2016, "Peer-to-Peer," Wikipedia.
[7]   Katherine Sagona-Stophel, "Bitcoin 101" [Online]. Available: http://www.trssllc.com/wp-
        content/uploads/2013/05/White_Paper_Bitcoin_101.pdf. [Accessed: 12-Jan-2017].
[8]   Bitcoin Wiki, "Hash" [Online]. Available: https://en.bitcoin.it/wiki/Hash. [Accessed: 14-Jan-
        2017].
[9]   Github, "Ethash Design Rationale," GitHub [Online]. Available:
        https://github.com/ethereum/wiki/wiki/Ethash-Design-Rationale. [Accessed: 19-Oct-2016].
[10]   Github, "Analysis of Ethash, Ethereum's Proof-of-Work Puzzle," GitHub [Online]. Available:
        https://github.com/LeastAuthority/ethereum-analyses. [Accessed: 15-Jan-2017].
[11]   bitcoinmining.com, "Learn about Bitcoin Mining Hardware" [Online]. Available:
        https://www.bitcoinmining.com/bitcoin-mining-hardware/. [Accessed: 15-Jan-2017].
[12]   Github, "Ethash," GitHub [Online]. Available: https://github.com/ethereum/wiki/wiki/Ethash.
        [Accessed: 15-Jan-2017].
[13]   Bitcoin Wiki, "Controlled Supply" [Online]. Available:
        https://en.bitcoin.it/wiki/Controlled_supply. [Accessed: 15-Jan-2017].
[14]   Wikipedia, the free encyclopedia, 2017, "Bitcoin," Wikipedia.
[15]   ethereum.org, "What Is Ether" [Online]. Available: https://www.ethereum.org/ether.
        [Accessed: 14-Jan-2017].
[16]   coinmarketcap.com, "Ethereum (ETH) Price, Charts, and Info" [Online]. Available:
        https://coinmarketcap.com/currencies/ethereum/#markets. [Accessed: 05-Feb-2017].
[17]   Poloniex, "Poloniex - Bitcoin/Cryptocurrency Exchange - Media Kit" [Online]. Available:
        https://poloniex.com/media-kit. [Accessed: 05-Feb-2017].
[18]   Kraken, "Kraken | Buy, Sell and Margin Trade Bitcoin (BTC) and Ethereum (ETH) - About"
        [Online]. Available: https://www.kraken.com/en-us/about. [Accessed: 05-Feb-2017].
[19]   CoinDesk, 2016, "Bitfinex Examined: Inside the Troubled Bitcoin Exchange's History,"
        CoinDesk [Online]. Available: http://www.coindesk.com/bitfinex-examined-bitcoin-exchange/.
        [Accessed: 05-Feb-2017].
[20]   JP Buntix, "Top 5 Cryptocurrencies That Can't Be Mined," The Merkle.
[21]   Dwarfpool, "DwarfPool" [Online]. Available: https://dwarfpool.com/eth. [Accessed: 05-Feb-
        2017].
[22]   Etherscan, "Ethereum Top Miner Stats" [Online]. Available:
        https://etherscan.io/stat/miner?range=7&blocktype=blocks. [Accessed: 05-Feb-2017].
[23]   Bitcoin Wiki, "Buying Bitcoins (the Newbie Version)" [Online]. Available:
        https://en.bitcoin.it/wiki/Buying_Bitcoins_(the_newbie_version). [Accessed: 08-Feb-2017].
[24]   expedia.com, "Bitcoin Terms & Conditions" [Online]. Available:
        http://www.expedia.com/Checkout/BitcoinTermsAndConditions. [Accessed: 08-Feb-2017].
[25]   cheapair.com, "What Forms of Payment Do You Accept? | Help."

[26] airBaltic, "Alternative Payment Options - Payment Options | airBaltic" [Online]. Available:
      https://www.airbaltic.com/en/alternative-payment. [Accessed: 08-Feb-2017].
[27] Microsoft, "BitcoinHowTo" [Online]. Available:
      https://commerce.microsoft.com/PaymentHub/Help/Right?helppagename=CSV_BitcoinHowTo
      .htm. [Accessed: 08-Feb-2017].
[28] Newegg.com, "BITCOIN ACCEPTED" [Online]. Available: https://www.newegg.com/bitcoin.
      [Accessed: 08-Feb-2017].
[29] 99 Bitcoins, 2016, "Who Accepts Bitcoins As Payment? List of Companies," 99 Bitcoins.
[30] blockchain.info, "Bitcoin Blockchain Wallet Users" [Online]. Available:
      https://blockchain.info/charts/my-wallet-n-users. [Accessed: 09-Feb-2017].
[31] Dan Cummings, "Use Cases Of Ethereum In Different Sectors 2016," ETHNews.com [Online].
      Available: https://www.ethnews.com/use-cases-of-ethereum-in-different-sectors-2016.
      [Accessed: 06-Apr-2017].
[32] Lester Coleman, 2016, "Banks Still Closing Accounts Over Bitcoin Activity," CryptoCoinsNews.
[33] "List of Bitcoin Hostile (and Friendly) Banks" [Online]. Available:
      https://bitcointalk.org/index.php?topic=264679.0. [Accessed: 09-Feb-2017].
[34] Wikipedia, the free encyclopedia, 2017, "Money Laundering," Wikipedia.
[35] Wikipedia, the free encyclopedia, 2017, "Know Your Customer," Wikipedia.
[36] AUSTRAC, 2014, "Customer Due Diligence" [Online]. Available:
      http://www.austrac.gov.au/businesses/obligations-and-compliance/customer-due-diligence.
      [Accessed: 09-Feb-2017].
[37] Jon Southurst, 2014, "The Real Reason Banks Don't Like Bitcoin," CoinDesk [Online].
      Available: http://www.coindesk.com/real-reason-banks-dont-like-bitcoin/. [Accessed: 09-Feb-
      2017].
[38] FinCEN, "Mission | FinCEN.gov" [Online]. Available: https://www.fincen.gov/about/mission.
      [Accessed: 09-Feb-2017].
[39] HG.org, "What Is the Threat of Money Laundering Associated with Bitcoin?" [Online].
      Available: https://www.hg.org/article.asp?id=31835. [Accessed: 09-Feb-2017].

Chapter 2

Basic knowledge of computer hardware, things you need to know before you start your mining business.

2. Hardware

Computer hardware consists of physical components that create a computer system or a Personal Computer (PC). The major computer components are:

2.1. CPU

The CPU (central processing unit) is the brain of a computer—the electronic circuitry within a computer that carries out the instructions of a computer program by performing the basic arithmetic, logical, control and input/output (I/O) operations specified by the instructions [1].

The CPU is connected to the motherboard through the designated CPU socket. Each generation of CPU has a different placement socket as the CPU requires different physical circuits that interact with it. For instance, the 5th generation Intel processors use the **LGA 1150** socket, which is also known as Socket H3 [2], and the 6th generation use the **LGA 1151** socket. Socket FM2+ (FM2b) is a CPU socket used by AMD's desktop "Kaveri" APUs [3] and **AM3+** is a modification of the AM3 Socket designed for CPUs, which uses the AMD Bulldozer microarchitecture and retains compatibility with AM3 [4].

In a GPU mining rig or Ethereum mining rig, the CPU doesn't play an important role as the mining is done by the GPUs and the CPU stays idle most of the time. So, a low-powered and relatively cheap CPU would be adequate.

Tips on buying a CPU for an Ethereum mining rig:

1. *The CPU should be low powered and have the minimum TDP[a] possible, as the CPU itself consumes power and dissipates heat even when it's idle. Having a lower TDP[5] saves some energy and reduces heat generation.*
2. *CPUs with more than two physical cores are not necessary for mining purposes. Spending money on something that is more powerful than a dual core Intel CPU or a quad core AMD CPU is wasting money. The best Intel options are the Pentium and Celeron series, and the best AMD options are Athlons.*

---

[a] The thermal design power (TDP), sometimes called thermal design point, is the maximum amount of heat generated by a computer chip or component (often the CPU or GPU) that the cooling system in a computer is designed to dissipate in typical operation.

3. The CPU must be compatible with the chosen motherboard. Usually, selection of the CPU is of least importance on a GPU mining rig. If you are going to buy a brand-new CPU, Intel sockets older than 1151 or 1150 (Gen. 4*th*) are not recommended because of their excessive electrical consumption compared with the 5*th*, 6*th*, and 7*th* Intel chipsets. AMD platforms are currently out of date, having been produced since 2012. The new Zen technology will be available in 2017, so buying a new AMD base system is not recommended at present unless you are offered a special price.

4. So, the CPU must be purchased after deciding about the motherboard. Always remember in a GPU mining rig, first we decide about the number and model of the GPU; after that we choose the right motherboard, then CPU and then the required PSU.

5. A price of ~$40 would be appropriate for the Intel 1150 socket, Intel Celeron **G1840** Dual Core CPU or similar CPU.

The recommended CPU with an Intel 1151 socket is Celeron **G3900** and this has a similar specification and price to the G1840.

2.2. Motherboard or Mainboard

The motherboard [6] is the main printed circuit board (PCB) of a computer on which all of the internal computer components are installed. Its purpose is to create a communicative platform for all of the computer hardware. A typical computer motherboard has a place for the CPU, RAM and GPU through different designated slots. Storage devices such as SSD, HDD and other drives usually connect through SATA (on most PCs) ports and cables or on new motherboards through a M.2 slot.

We are not concerned in detail with the features and capabilities of a motherboard in a mining rig. There are only two features that are important:

1. The number of available PCIE slots to accommodate the GPUs.
2. The chipset and variation of the motherboard—what type of CPU and RAM can be supported.

Motherboards come in different sizes, but in a GPU mining rig, we usually use a full-size ATX motherboard that has 4 to 6 available PCIE slots[2].

Tips on buying a Motherboard for an Ethereum mining rig

1. *The more PCIE slots, the better. As the GPUs are connected to the motherboard through PCIE slots, the motherboard must have at least the same number of available PCIE slots as the desired number of GPUs in your system. In a mining rig, even a PCIE X1 works fine and offers enough bandwidth for GPU mining. So, the total number of available PCIE slots is a combination of all the PCIE slots types. Some motherboards have a combination of X16, X8, X4 and X1. It's always better to get a motherboard that has one or more available PCIE slots more than you require at the moment as this allows you to add more GPUs in the future if you need to.*
2. *Buy the newest equipment that you can. If you are planning to build a new system, Intel, 1150 and 1151 sockets are recommended. At the moment, there may be some good deals on the market for 1150 motherboards. This motherboard works with the cheaper DDR3 RAM types whereas the 1151 motherboard usually requires DDR4 RAM types (there are only a few 1151 motherboards that work with DDR3). However, 1151 and the 6thgeneration Intel CPUs are slightly more efficient.*

---

[2] This book is not intended to explain everything about hardware, but just to give the essential information. If you want more information. you can find it online without difficulty. The points which I have highlighted are important for building a GPU mining rig.

2.3. Physical memory or RAM

Random access memory (RAM) is the best-known form of computer memory [7]. The RAM is connected through motherboard memory slots, and it is the computer's temporary fast working storage place. When a computer loads, and reads a program, all the data are transferred and stored in the memory. The data are then sent to be processed by the CPU and GPU, and after processing, the data are again stored back in the RAM [8]. So, this memory is a temporary buffer that lets data queue there and prepare for the next stage.

In a GPU mining rig, the RAM component is comparatively the least important of the internal components. Usually, 8 GB of memory is enough for a five to six GPU mining rig (although 4 GB may work fine!). The RAM selection should be compatible with the motherboard; older motherboards used to use DDR2, but AM3+, 1155, 1150 and a few 1151 socket motherboards use DDR3 memories. The 1151 or 6th generation Intel CPUs mostly use DDR4 RAMs. The speed of the RAM isn't important at all for mining purposes, so buying a cheaper option is better regardless of speed—1333 MHz and above does the job.

2.4. Storage devices, SSD, HDD, DVD drives, ...

A data storage device is a device for recording (storing) information (data) [9]. In a personal computer, the storage device is where the operating system, program's data and personal information are stored. The HDD (hard disk drive) has many solid rotating disks that record the data magnetically, and the SSD (solid state drive) contains memory chips and have no moving parts.

In a GPU mining rig, the storage device has two purposes: 1. Providing a running operating system, usually Microsoft Windows, Linux family or Mac OS., and 2. Allowing the mining program to be installed and run. In a network-mining or pool-mining system, a small amount of storage is required. But a solo-mining rig requires a pretty big storage capacity. The Current Blockchain Size of Ethereum in June 2016 was more than 60 GB with some mining clients (mining programs) and is expected to grow by more than 5 GB per month [10].

Tips on buying a Storage Drive for an Ethereum mining rig

1. Use a small SSD in pool mining. An SSD is more reliable and harder to break as it does not have any moving parts that eventually will wear out. Some of the SSDs can handle up to 700 Terabytes of writing before they die [11]. A good 64 GB or 128 GB SSD, which now costs around $50—128 GB, is adequate for an operating system and mining program in a pool-mining application.
2. Use a 1 TB HDD in a solo-mining rig. A reliable 1 TB HDD is more than enough for a mining rig. Furthermore, a 1 TB HDD is usually the minimum capacity that can be bought these days. A 1 TB HDD costs around $50. I recommend Samsung 2.5-Inch 120 GB 850 EVO and SanDisk SSD Plus 120 GB.

3. Don't buy used storage when the rig is important for you! If the storage fails, the mining operation will stop and it will take time to recover the system. This failure is unlike the breakdown of the other components, such as GPUs, PSU, CPU, RAM. Even the motherboard can be replaced rather quickly without a significant loss in operating time. The operating system and mining software are installed on the storage device, and usually there is only one physical drive being used on a mining rig (unlike a server computer which utilizes multiple drives as the backup). So, if the mining rig is running 24/7, or operated remotely without regular supervision, it is vital that you use a reliable and therefore new storage—second-hand HDDs or SDDs should be totally avoided.

2.5. GPU or VGA

The GPU (Graphics Processing Unit) is a computer component specialized for display functions. The GPU renders images, animations and videos for the computer's screen. GPUs are located on plug-in cards and are placed in PCI Express [12]. There are two major producers of video cards or GPUs—Nvidia with about 65% of the discrete GPU-market share in the second quarter of 2016, and AMD with 35% of the market [13]. A graphics card is the most important part in a GPU mining rig while all of the hard work and mining tasks are done by the GPU rendering power (unlike a regular desktop or workstation computer in which the CPU is also very active and important).

A mining software or client utilizes 100% of the GPU power and therefore the maximum designed TDP[3] of the GPU would be reached. This matter makes the GPU consume its maximum designed electrical energy and consequently dissipates this consumed energy in the form of heat. If the TDP were lower, the electrical power consumption and generated heat would also be lower. However, in a particular generation of GPU (when the manufacturing technology and design are the same), for instance, in AMD Radeon RX 400s series (RX 480: 150 watts, RX 470: 120 watts and RX 460: 75 [14]), a lower TDP would mean a lower graphical computational power. Two different generations of GPUs may therefore have different TDP design but similar computational power. As the production technology advances and microcontrollers become smaller and more optimized, they require less energy to do the same operation. What could be processed in a certain time with a 250 watt GPU in 2014, may be achieved with a newer GPU with 150 watts of TDP in 2016.

2.5.1. Flops and performance per watt

According to Wikipedia "In computing, FLOPS or flops (an acronym for Floating-points Operations Per Second) is a measure of computer performance, useful in fields of scientific calculations that make heavy use of floating-point calculations." For such cases, it is a more accurate measure than the generic instructions per second [15] so stronger GPUs have higher flops. For instance, new AMD GPUs Radeon RX 480, RX 470 and RX 460 have 5.8, 4.9 and 2.2 teraflops. **The best GPUs are those that have high flops ratings with low TDPs.** The performance per watt is calculated by dividing the number of flops by the TDP; the higher the resulting number, the higher the efficiency. Indeed, the number of flops does not necessarily represent the real performance of the GPU in a GPU mining client or in a real-world scenario but it

---

[3] Again: The thermal design power (TDP), sometimes called thermal design point, is the maximum amount of heat generated by a computer chip or component (often the CPU or GPU) that the cooling system in a computer is designed to dissipate in typical operation.

determines the potential of the GPU's computational power based on the number of chipset transistors and the manufacturer's design.

Figure 1 - Head of RTG (Radeon Technologies Group) Raja Koduri was pictured holding a Vega chip during CES 2017, AMD Vega GPU speculates to have 12 TFLOPS of computation power. Link of picture is here!

As the chips and circuit boards become smaller, they require a lower voltage and power to operate. The process technology is the particular manufacturing method used to make silicon chips, which is measured by how small the transistor is. The size of a manufactured transistor is measured in nanometers (1 nanometer = one billionth of a meter). In 2006, the 65 nm (nanometers) technology was being used. Accordingly, Intel Core 2 CPU, AMD Turion 64 X2 CPU and NVIDIA GeForce 8800GT GPU were manufactured with 65-nm technology [16]. The Matsushita company and Intel started mass-producing 45-nm chips in the late 2007, and AMD started production of 45-nm chips in the late 2008[17]. This technology was utilized in products such as the Intel first generation Core i7 and Core i5 series of processors (such as i5 750), and AMD Phenom II processors (six core CPUs such a 1055T). All AMD R9 series of desktop GPUs, including R9 Nano and R9 Fury, use 28-nm GPU architectures [18]. The 28-nm process was introduced in 2012; it was also used in the Nvidia 700 series of GPU desktops and even in the dual GPU GeForce GTX Titan Z in March 2014 [19]. The successor of the 700 series, the 900 series, also was produced with a 28-nm GPU architecture [20]. However, in the GeForce 10 series, Nvidia uses a 16-nm GPU architecture [21]. AMD currently uses the new Polaris architecture and makes the Radeon RX 400 series of GPUs with the latest FinFET 14-nm process (technology) [22]. According to AMD, the RX 480 uses a lower energy consumption for the GPU of up to 40% [23].

Typical Use Scenario		R9 390	RX 480	Percent (%)
Operating State	Hours Per Day	Annual Electricity Use (kWh)	Annual Electricity Use (kWh)	Change in Annual kWh from R9 390 to RX 480
Active Gaming (3DMark 2013 loop)	4.4	642.4	385.4	-40%
Video Streaming (1080p, YouTube/Netflix)	1.6	88.2	73.6	-17%
Web Browsing (Manual or Peacekeeper benchmark)	2.0	87.6	58.4	-33%
Long Idle (standby)	3.0	33.0	33.3	1%
Short Idle (active hard drive)	1.0	69.1	73.6	6%
Off	6.0	3.0	3.0	0%
Sleep	6.0	5.8	5.8	0%
Annual Electricity Use (kwh)		929	633	-32%

Figure 2 – Comparison of AMD GPUs in Carbon footprint study by AMD

In April 2017, AMD has released 500s series of graphics card which use the same 14nm FinFET manufacturing process, but with improvement in manufacturing process, 500s series GPUs achieve higher GPU core clock speeds. Radeon RX 580 and 570 have 5%-10% higher core stock clocks than 400s counterparts. But unfortunately, this improvement is achieved by bumping up the core voltage of the GPU and therefore it has resulted on higher power consumption of the cards. Radeon RX 580 has TDP of 185 W comparing to 150 W of RX 480, and RX 570 has TDP of 150 W comparing to 120 W of RX 470. As a result, as you can find on next table, the efficiency of the 500s series GPU are much worse the 400s series. So, 500s cards have inferior performance per watt ratio, and therefore this matter, makes them less suitable for a GPU mining rig.

The charts and table below show the difference in teraflops and designed TDPs between the AMD Radeon R9 and RX series. The performance per watt was calculated from the expression (TFLOPS X 100)/TDP—the higher value, the better. The approximate price of the GPUs according to www.amazon.de in Euro is given for comparison purposes and the price/performance value is calculated by dividing price/performance per watt—the lower the value, the better.

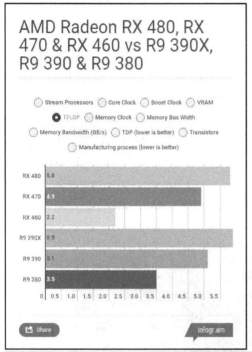

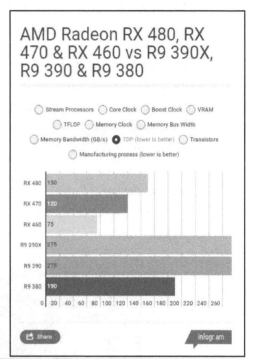

AMD GPU Showdown					
	TFLOPS	TDP (watt)	Performance per Watt (higher is better)	Lowest Price	Price/Performance (lower is better)
RX 580	6.17	185	3.3	$ 249.99	74.96
RX 570	5.1	150	3.4	$ 199.99	58.82
RX 560	2.6	75	3.5	$ 109.99	31.73
RX 550	1.2	65	1.8	$ 79.90	43.28
RX 480	5.8	150	3.9	$ 229.99	59.48
RX 470	4.9	120	4.1	$ 189.00	46.29
RX 460	2.2	75	2.9	$ 89.99	30.68
R9 380	3.5	190	1.8	$ 183.00	99.34
R9 380X	4	190	2.1	$ 217.00	103.08
R9 390	5.1	275	1.9	$ 319.00	172.01
R9 390X	5.9	275	2.1	$ 355.00	165.47
R9 Nano	8.1	175	4.6	$ 523.00	112.99
R9 Fury	7.1	275	2.6	$ 355.00	137.50
R9 Fury X	8.6	275	3.1	$ 479.00	153.17

2.5.2. Cooling design of GPU

GPUs differ in many ways. In a GPU mining rig, the second most important aspect of the GPU after its computational power or FLOPS, is the "cooling design or cooling solution". A GPU generates a lot of heat, which needs to be dissipated to keep the core chip and components below the design values. In chapter 3, I explain in detail about heat generation and its dissipation and the life of the components. I also discuss in detail cooling designs. Here, I cover them briefly.

GPUs are equipped with two types of coolers or fans: 1. the blower-style or turbine and 2. the open-air style. In the first type, there is a single centrifugal fan usually placed at the end of the card where usually the power connecters are placed. This fan sucks the air inside a shroud and blows it throw a heatsink which is usually connected with the main chipset of GPU, VRMs and memory chips of GPU. The warm air is emitted from the GPU head. In the second type, there are multiple axial fans which blow air downwards to the designated heatsink which is connected to the GPU components, and the warmed air is exhausted to the surroundings, usually inside the computer case.

Figure 3 - Radeon RX 480 reference design (blower design), blue arrow shows the intake air direction and red arrow shows the warm air direction coming out of the card.

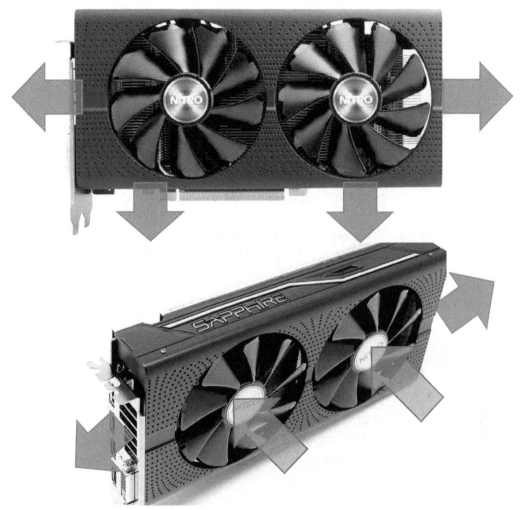

Figure 4 - Pictures shows the Radeon Sapphire RX 480 8GB Nitro+, with two axial intake fans . Thewarm air would be exhausted from different directions.

Tips on buying a GPU for a mining rig

1.   **GPUs with 3 GB RAM or more.** At the moment, Ethereum mining clients require more than 2 GB of available memory in the GPU. GPUs with 2 GB can't mine directly and would need to be modified on the client [24], but eventually the amount of memory will not be enough. Thus, the DAG started at 1 GB at the time of the Frontier launch, and increased by approximately 0.73 times per year [25]. The size is therefore roughly 1.35

GB as of mid-January 2016. Following the same crude approximation: the 2 GB threshold would have been reached around mid-December 2016 and the 3 GB threshold mid-April 2018. The 4 GB threshold would be reached around mid-September 2019 [26]. At the moment, the only new generation of GPUs from AMD that has 2 GB variants is RX 460, so you will need to avoid buying that card for Ethereum mining purposes. However, the 4 GB variant works fine.

2. *Always buy a GPU with an open-air design.*

3. *Buy a GPU with a backplate.* As of today, the price of a card with or without the backplate are very similar. A backplate offers extra protection, rigidity and heat dissipation options.

4. *Always buy the same model and same brand of a GPU for a mining rig.* Do not mix different brands. In my experience, the new AMD RX 400 series have problems with mining clients while working on different frequencies and different fan speeds. Often, I found that controlling the frequency and fan speed using software like "MSI after Burner", results in crashes or freezing of the system[4].

5. *Be on the lookout for local sales and special offers.* From time to time, graphics cards are sold at a discounted price online, but unfortunately most of the offers are in the USA. For instance, on newegg.com, at the end of February 2017, you could buy an RX 480 ARMOR 4G OC for $164.99 after a $20.00 rebate, which is almost $50 lower than regular price.

2.6. Input devices, including keyboard, mouse, scanner, etc.

A mining rig requires a mouse and keyboard for the initial setup and, later on, in order to undertake updates and maintenance. However, on a remotely controlled system, a mouse and keyboard aren't necessary, but as they cost virtually nothing and consume less than a watt of power, it does not matter if they are connected to a remotely controlled system.

2.7. Display monitor

---

[4] To read more please read chapters 3 and 5, which deal specially with building a GPU mining rig

As with the keyboard and mouse, a monitor is required to set up the mining rig and to do on-site maintenance and upgrades. However, a 20" LED or LCD monitor can consume up to 30 watthours [27], so when it is not necessary, monitors should be switched off manually. They should not however be put into sleep mode as this may interfere with mining operations. Often the mining system is set to remain awake and use 100% of the system's resources, so setting a sleep time for hard drives or monitors is not recommended.

2.8. Output devices including printer, speaker, etc.

An Ethereum mining system does not require an extra output device such as a printer or speaker, unless it is being used as a daily computer too.

2.9. Computer Case

This is the enclosure that contains the computer components. It excludes the input and output devices such as the monitor, speaker, mouse and keyboard. The computer case is made of metal, plastics or any other material that is rigid enough to hold the components and offer enough protection. You will need to remember in a professional GPU mining rig that usually the computer chassis has an open-air design unlike the typical closed-air system of a normal computer case. I explain in detail in Chapter 5 how to build a GPU mining rig.

The computer case has several functions:

1. Holding the components and keeping them secure. Computer components are placed in a computer case, which holds them together and provides a rigid base to keep them secure. The motherboard and internal computer components usually have bare electronic parts that should not be touched.
2. Cooling of the hardware. The electrical energy used by the computer eventually finishes up as heat. So, when a computer uses 1000 watthours of electricity, it would generate 1000 watthours of heat. The generated heat is dissipated by cooling fans which usually are placed inside the computer case. In addition, the case directs the path of the airstream.
3. Appearance of the computer system. For many computer enthusiasts, the appearance of the computer plays a significant role, as is the case with cars.
4. Filtering the dust. Most modern computer cases are equipped with cleanable dust filters right in front of the intake fan. Keeping the components of the computer clean, helps to prolong the life of the moving parts like the GPU

fan and case-cooling fans. Accumulated dirt and dust between the heatsink fins of the CPU, GPU and PSU can affect their cooling.

Tips on buying a computer case for a mining rig

1. Most of the well-built GPU mining rigs with five or six GPUs use open-air design as the case or chassis, see **Chapter 5** to learn more about this.

2. **Use a quiet intake fan⁵**, as your system runs 24/7, if the mining rig in not placed in an isolated area. Some of the original case fans are noisy when they run at high speed. Pay extra attention to the fans that are already installed in the case, if you have decided not to replace the original case fans.

3. **A dust filter is a must.** As said earlier, most computer cases are equipped with dust filters. For a system that runs all the time, dust is an enemy of a GPU mining rig. The dusts filter should be placed on the intake path, and be easily removed and cleaned.

4. **The bigger, the better.** Usually a mining rig with up to **four** GPUs, can be built into a computer case, but this is not ideal for more than **two** GPUs. Why? Because 1. an ordinary computer case is not designed to accommodate so many GPUs, 2. heat dissipation would be troublesome as the GPUs will be placed tightly together, and 3. maintenance and changes are more difficult to undertake in a confined space.

---

⁵ Please pay attention to this tip if you build a GPU mining rig in a small closed-air chassis. Read more in Chapter 5.

2.10.   Power Supply Unit (PSU)

A power supply unit (or PSU) converts the mains AC electricity (alternative current) to a low-voltage regulated DC power supply for the internal components of a computer [28]. The most modern desktop personal computer power supplies conform to the ATX[6] specification [29], which covers both the form factor (shape and size of the PSU) and voltage tolerances. While an ATX power supply is connected to the mains supply, it always provides a 5-volt standby (5VSB) voltage so that the standby functions on the computer and certain peripherals are powered. ATX power supplies are turned on and off by a signal from the motherboard. They also provide a signal to the motherboard to indicate when the DC voltages are within specification, so that the computer is able to safely power up and boot.

Many ATX PSUs which are available to buy, do comply with the ATX standard, revision 2.31, which was established in mid-2008. The compliant standard is always mentioned on the product page, in the product's details or in the description section. The latest standard revision of ATX PSU is the "Specific Guidelines version 2.4", which was introduced in April 2013 [30] (not so new!)

Figure 5 - This is the EVGA SuperNOVA 1000 P2 Power Supply, with an efficiency of 80 Platinum. It will set you back ~$180, and is one of the best choices for a GPU mining rig, link is here!

---

[6] ATX (Advanced Technology eXtended) is a motherboard configuration specification developed by **Intel** in 1997. It was the first major change in desktop computer enclosure, motherboard and power supply design in many years, improving standardization and interchangeability of parts. The specification defines the key mechanical dimensions, mounting point, I/O panel, power and connector interfaces between a computer case, a motherboard and a power supply.

Figure 6 - This is HX Series™ HX1000 — 1000 Watt 80 PLUS® Platinum. It costs ~$199. It is a reliable and efficient PSU for a power demanding system, link is here!

What are the main factors of a PSU that a Ethereum mining rig builder should pay attention to?

2.10.1. **The output power**. This is the most important factor of a PSU for a mining rig. It should be able to supply enough power to the GPUs. How much power do you need? This is mainly dependent on the number of GPUs that do the mining. Almost every PSU manufactures has a "Power Supply Calculator" page that helps you to choose a suitable PSU for your job, See the following websites: Cooler Master [31], Be Quiet! [32], Outer Vision [33] or Corsair PSU Finder [34]. However, the easiest way is to calculate the required power of your PSU for a **modern new** (using only GPUs from 2016 or later and hardware like AMD Radeon RX 480) Ethereum rig as follow:

- Minimum PSU requirement: 150 watts multiplied by the number of GPUs

- Recommended PSU requirement: 200 watts multiplied by the number of GPUs

2.10.2. **Number of PCIE power connectors.** As a PCIE power connector is required to supply power to the GPU, a mining rig needs special attention. Based on the GPU selection, each GPU may require different power requirement, and a different number of PCIE connectors with 6 or 8 pins of powerlines. For instance, the original AMD Radeon RX 480 Reference design requires only a single 6-pin PCIE connector while most of AMD Radeon RX 480s of different brands, require a single 8-pin connector. So, if a GPU mining rig uses five AMD RX 480 aftermarket brands (such as MSI, ASUS, Sapphire, XFX,) it will need four PCIE 8-pin power connectors. Some of the high-wattage PSUs do not have enough PCIE lines and therefore selection of the PSU needs to be undertaken with care.

2.10.3. Efficiency and ATX standards.

Most PSUs are certified to 80 PLUS and Intel ATX standards. The 80 PLUS® performance specification requires power supplies for computers and servers to have 80% or greater energy efficiency at 10, 20, 50 and 100% of the rated load with a true power factor of 0.9 or higher [35]. When a 1000 W power supply complies with 80 Plus, it would take 1250 W of electricity to provide the required 1000 W (i.e. 80% of 1250 W), but a 1000 W PSU which complies with 80 Plus Gold requires 1150 W (in countries with 115 V) and 1112 W for the Titanium series. In a mining rig, usually the PSU operates between 85–95% of the load all the time, so the efficiency at 100 % load is the most important factor to consider [36].

Table 1 - This table shows the comparison between different 80 standards of the PSU. The most important column to be watched on a GPU mining rig is the efficiency above 80% utilization of the PSU. This would always work in a mining rig.

Efficiency level certifications

80 Plus test type	115V internal non-redundant				230V internal redundant				230V EU internal non-redundant			
Percentage of rated load	10%	20%	50%	100%	10%	20%	50%	100%	10%	20%	50%	100%
80 Plus		80%	80%	80%						82%	85%	82%
80 Plus Bronze		82%	85%	82%		81%	85%	81%		85%	88%	85%
80 Plus Silver		85%	88%	85%		85%	89%	85%		87%	90%	87%
80 Plus Gold		87%	90%	87%		88%	92%	88%		90%	92%	89%
80 Plus Platinum		90%	92%	89%		90%	94%	91%		92%	94%	90%
80 Plus Titanium	90%	92%	94%	90%	90%	94%	96%	91%	90%	94%	96%	94%

(Recommended buying range — spanning 80 Plus through 80 Plus Gold)

As mentioned earlier, the current Intel ATX standard is 2.4. However, many PSUs are still compatible with the older revision of 2.31.

2.10.4. Price per watt. At the moment, the price of 80 Plus and 80 Plus bronze is about 10 watts per dollar. A good branded PSU with 1000 W output can be found for around $100 (or €100), and to get an 80 Plus Gold, the price shifts to about 4–6 watts per dollar as it normally costs more than $150. However, the cost of paying for the extra efficiency can be recovered within a mining year. How? Let's put it in real example:

An Ethereum mining rig with the following components:

- Motherboard: Asrock B150A-X1 Intel 1151

- CPU: Intel Celeron G3900 2.8 GHz LGA1151 2 MB 51W TDP

- RAM: Crucial 8 GB CL16 DDR4 DIMM Memory Module

- PSU: Thermaltake Toughpower Grand 1050 W

- GPU: 5 units of AMD Radeon RX 480 4 GB

The price of an 80 Plus Gold PSU was about $170 in www.newegg.com in Oct. 2016 [37]. in The extra efficiency that Gold offers compared to Bronze, is 87% as against 82% at 90% power utilization, which is:

$$the\ power\ saving = (\frac{1050\ W}{82\%} - \frac{1050\ W}{87\%})\ X\ 90\%\ utilization\ of\ PSU\ while\ mining = 66.6\ W$$

The cost of 66.6 W of electricity consumption 24/7 in a year is $69 with an average cost of $0.12/kWh. So, the extra $70 (i.e. the difference between $100 and $170) will be recovered within the first year of a mining operation[7].

---

[7] For more information, go to the article "Is it worth investing in a high-efficiency power supply by Joel Hruska. The link is here!

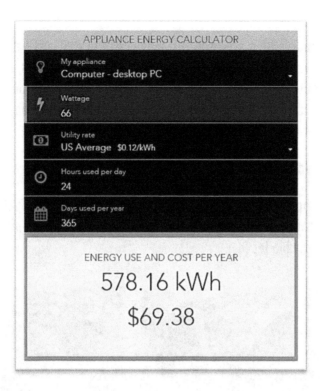

Figure 7 - Cost of the 66 watthours of energy in a year in the United States, calculated using the energy calculator from U.S. department of Energy, link is here!

However, from Gold to Titanium, the gain gets smaller and the price may soar up to 200%. Thus, the recommended buying range is from 80 Plus to 80 Plus Gold in most conditions. But do the calculations yourself for your own system before you decide to buy, and please read more in the **Chapters 4** and **5**.

2.10.5. Noise from the PSU. During operation, the PSU also generates heat. For instance, the energy lost by a 1000 W, 80 Plus Gold PSU is 150 W and the resulting heat needs to be dissipated. In a mining rig, as the PSU runs at its maximum utilization most of the time, the cooling fans of the PSU also run at their maximum speed. Some PSU fans are very noisy when they run at maximum speed, and this needs to be taken into account if the generated noise of the mining rig is an important consideration. Most manufacturers offer some information about the maximum noise levels of their PSUs with their product information details.

However, in a big mining farm with so many open-air systems, the noise from the PSUs is generally swamped by the noise of the GPUs (see chapter 5).

2.11. Cooling Fans

Fans or computer fans are used for active cooling [38]. Active cooling of a computer usually involves transferring heat to air, water or other liquids, and moving the heated medium to outside of the case [39]. If a particular component doesn't generate too much heat, passive cooling can be used. For instance, most motherboard VRMs, chipsets and RAMs use passive cooling systems.

2.12. Types and main design

Most computers fans are **Axial** fans. An axial fan increases the pressure of the air flowing through it. The blades of the axial flow fans force air to move parallel to the shaft of the blades [40].

Figure 8 – A picture of a Corsair Air Series 120 mm PWM High Performance Edition High Static Pressure Fan, an example of axial computer fan

Figure 9 – A picture of a typical workshop and industrial axial fans, of different sizes, from 300 to 3800 CFM.

The other type of computer fan is the centrifugal type, often called blowers. The pressure of an incoming airstream is increased by a fan wheel, a series of blades mounted on a circular hub. Centrifugal fans move air radially, the direction of the outward flowing air is changed; it is usually at 90° to the direction of the incoming air [41]. These types are commonly used in GPUs, laptops and compact desktop machines, all-in-one computers, printers, projectors, etc. where there is not enough space for air movement within the casing of the components[8].

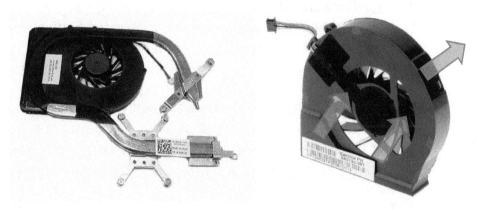

Figure 10 – The picture on the left shows a laptop cooling fan with attached cooling pipes, the picture on the right shows the direction of airflow from a centrifugal fan.

2.13. Features of a computer fan (only axial)

- **Size.** The standard computer fan sizes are 80, 90, 120, 140 and 200 millimeters. The most common size is 120 mm. However, in a GPU mining rig with five or six GPUs, computer fans alone don't provide enough airflow, and the mining rig requires additional fans. More is said about this in Chapter 5.

- **PWM or non-PWM.** Pulse-width modulation (PWM) is a common method of controlling computer fans. A PWM-capable fan is usually connected to a 4-pin connector (pinout: ground, +12 V, sense output from fan and control input) [42]. Non-PWM fans have 3-pin connectors and usually they are called "computer case fan" while they run only at a constant speed. Although even non-PWM fans can be controlled by altering the 12 V DC input using a fan controller or motherboard, not all motherboards are capable of altering the fan voltage. For

---

[8] To read more about this topic, please refer to the article "Axial vs. Centrifugal Fans" link is <u>here</u>!

instance, a motherboard cannot deliver 10 V to a fan header as it can only deliver a total of 12 V.

- **Noise.** Noise is inevitably created by the contact of the fan blades with air. Usually, the maximum noise level of a fan is mentioned in the product data sheet in terms of decibels or sones.

- **Bearing type.** A computer fan consists of fan blades, a hub, an electromotor and bearings. There are many different designs of bearing—ball bearings, sliding bearings, hydro-pressure bearings, magnetic levitated bearings and so on. Bearing design has a direct effect on the life of the fan and noise which is generated by the fan.

- **Airflow and static pressure.** Airflow fans are those that have high airflows (high CFM) when there is little or no restriction. In a computer case, intake and exhaust fans are usually airflow fans. Static pressure fans offer good airflow when there is an obstacle such as radiator or dust filter restricting the flow.

  Airflow fans tend to have a larger number and thinner blades than pressure fans [43]. These are the right type of fans for a GPU mining [44], when there is no radiator or restricted closed-case chassis as is the case in most GPU mining rigs.

RPM (Revolutions per minute) and relative power. One of the most understandable features of any fan is its RPM; how fast a fan rotates indicates other characteristics. For a particular fan, when the RPM is increased, the air pressure or flow and the noise increase. However, this is not necessarily the case with different fans—a higher RPM fan does not necessarily result in a higher airflow or noise. Some fans rotate at relatively low RPMs and produce a high airflow because of having a larger number of larger blades. Increasing the airflow of a particular fan requires more power. For instance, a Delta AFB1212ME fan with a blade thickness of 38 mm produces an airflow of 91.95 CFM at 2500 RPM, requires 3.24 watthours [45]. Its thinner brother, AFB1212H, with a blade thickness of 25 mm, produces 82.67 CFM at the same RPM and requires 2.65 watthours [46][9].

Tips on buying a computer fan for a mining rig

1. *Most of the tips can be read on Chapter 5, on building a GPU mining rig.*

---

[9] More on the choice of fans in Chapter 5.

2. In a GPU mining rig, we should use airflow rather than static pressure fans.

3. If noise isn't a problem, the recommended fans are those which have higher CFMs and operate up to 4000 RPM.

4. Never connect a high-RPM & high-wattage fan to a motherboard fan header, as it may damage the motherboard because of the high-power drain. Always use a fan controller that can provide up to 3 amps to a fan header.

5. You will require an extra 100–150 CFM for each GPU of your open-air mining rig. Read more about this in Chapters 3, and 5.

6. A cooling solution with 120 mm high-RPM computer fans and a fan controller generally costs less than an industrial solution. High-RPM fans usually cost ~$15–20 on Amazon, so for a 5–6 GPU mining rig, the total system may cost around $100.

7. If you are looking for a special type of fan, or a high performance one, I suggest that you look at the Delta Electronics website here. Delta has an enormous range of different types of fan in different sizes that are widely available on the webstores [47].

References

[1] Wikipedia, the free encyclopedia, 2016, "Central Processing Unit," Wikipedia [Online]. Available: https://en.wikipedia.org/w/index.php?title=Central_processing_unit&oldid=743975561. [Accessed: 13-Oct-2016].

[2] Wikipedia, the free encyclopedia, 2016, "LGA 1150," Wikipedia [Online]. Available: https://en.wikipedia.org/w/index.php?title=LGA_1150&oldid=716841627. [Accessed: 13-Oct-2016].

[3] Wikipedia, the free encyclopedia, 2016, "Socket FM2+," Wikipedia [Online]. Available: https://en.wikipedia.org/w/index.php?title=Socket_FM2%2B&oldid=735162133. [Accessed: 13-Oct-2016].

[4] 2016, "Socket AM3+," Wikipedia [Online]. Available: https://en.wikipedia.org/w/index.php?title=Socket_AM3%2B&oldid=734480062. [Accessed: 13-Oct-2016].

[5] Wikipedia, the free encyclopedia, 2016, "Thermal Design Power," Wikipedia [Online]. Available: https://en.wikipedia.org/w/index.php?title=Thermal_design_power&oldid=739448763. [Accessed: 15-Oct-2016].

[6] Wikipedia, the free encyclopedia, 2016, "Motherboard," Wikipedia [Online]. Available: https://en.wikipedia.org/w/index.php?title=Motherboard&oldid=743969926. [Accessed: 14-Oct-2016].

[7] HowStuffWorks, 2000, "How RAM Works," HowStuffWorks [Online]. Available: http://computer.howstuffworks.com/ram.htm. [Accessed: 14-Oct-2016].

[8] Wikipedia, the free encyclopedia, 2016, "Random-Access Memory," Wikipedia [Online]. Available: https://en.wikipedia.org/w/index.php?title=Random-access_memory&oldid=743439912. [Accessed: 14-Oct-2016].

[9] Wikipedia, the free encyclopedia, 2016, "Data Storage Device," Wikipedia [Online]. Available: https://en.wikipedia.org/w/index.php?title=Data_storage_device&oldid=739753882. [Accessed: 14-Oct-2016].

[10] Ethereum Stack Exchange, "Blockchain - What Are the Ethereum Disk Space Needs?" [Online]. Available: http://ethereum.stackexchange.com/questions/143/what-are-the-ethereum-disk-space-needs. [Accessed: 14-Oct-2016].

[11] techreport.com, "The SSD Endurance Experiment: They're All Dead," Tech Rep. [Online]. Available: http://techreport.com/review/27909/the-ssd-endurance-experiment-theyre-all-dead/4. [Accessed: 14-Oct-2016].

[12] PC Magazine Encyclopedia, "GPU Definition" [Online]. Available: http://www.pcmag.com/encyclopedia/term/43886/gpu. [Accessed: 15-Oct-2016].

[13] WCCFtech, 2016, "AMD Takes More GPU Market Share From Nvidia In Q1 2016 - Builds Momentum Ahead Of Polaris Launch," WCCFtech.

[14] Minasians, C., "Which AMD Polaris Card to Choose? The RX 480, 470 or 460. We Help You Decide.," PC Advis. [Online]. Available: http://www.pcadvisor.co.uk/feature/pc-components/amd-rx-480-vs-rx-470-vs-rx-460-3643619/. [Accessed: 15-Oct-2016].

[15] Wikipedia, the free encyclopedia, 2016, "FLOPS," Wikipedia.

[16] Wikipedia, the free encyclopedia, 2016, "65 Nanometer," Wikipedia.

[17] Wikipedia, the free encyclopedia, 2016, "45 Nanometer," Wikipedia.

[18] AMD, "Radeon™ R9 Series Graphics Cards | AMD" [Online]. Available: http://www.amd.com/en-us/products/graphics/desktop/r9. [Accessed: 17-Oct-2016].

[19] Wikipedia, the free encyclopedia, 2016, "GeForce 700 Series," Wikipedia.

[20] Wikipedia, the free encyclopedia, 2016, "GeForce 900 Series," Wikipedia.

[21] Wikipedia, the free encyclopedia, 2016, "GeForce 10 Series," Wikipedia.

[22] AMD, "Polaris Architecture" [Online]. Available: http://www.amd.com/en-us/innovations/software-technologies/radeon-polaris. [Accessed: 17-Oct-2016].

[23] AMD, "AMD Accelerates GPU Energy Efficiency for Gaming PCs" [Online]. Available: http://www.amd.com/Documents/polaris-carbon-footprint-study.pdf. [Accessed: 17-Oct-2016].

[24] Crypto Mining Blog, "How to Fix Ethminer Not-Working Issues on 2GB GPUs" [Online]. Available: http://cryptomining-blog.com/7606-how-to-fix-ethminer-not-working-issues-on-2gb-gpus/. [Accessed: 19-Oct-2016].

[25] Github, "Ethash Design Rationale," GitHub [Online]. Available: https://github.com/ethereum/wiki/wiki/Ethash-Design-Rationale. [Accessed: 19-Oct-2016].

[26] Ethereum Stack Exchange, "Mining - What Is the Current DAG Size? When Do We Expect to Hit GPU Limits? -" [Online]. Available: http://ethereum.stackexchange.com/questions/426/what-is-the-current-dag-size-when-do-we-expect-to-hit-gpu-limits. [Accessed: 19-Oct-2016].

[27] energyusecalculator.com, "Electricity Usage of an LED, LCD, Plasma, CRT TV or Computer Display - Energy Use Calculator" [Online]. Available: http://energyusecalculator.com/electricity_lcdleddisplay.htm. [Accessed: 17-Oct-2016].

[28] Wikipedia, the free encyclopedia, 2016, "Power Supply Unit (Computer)," Wikipedia.

[29] Wikipedia, the free encyclopedia, 2016, "ATX," Wikipedia.

[30] Intel Corporation, "Power Supply: Design Guide for Desktop Platform Form Factors, Revision 1.31" [Online]. Available: https://web.archive.org/web/20141021123124/http://cache-www.intel.com:80/cd/00/00/52/37/523796_523796.pdf. [Accessed: 20-Oct-2016].

[31] Cooler Master, "Cooler Master Power Supply Calculator" [Online]. Available: http://www.coolermaster.com/power-supply-calculator/. [Accessed: 20-Oct-2016].

[32] bequiet.com, "Power Supply Calculator - Calc for Silent PSUs of Be Quiet!" [Online]. Available: http://www.bequiet.com/en/psucalculator. [Accessed: 20-Oct-2016].

[33] outervision.com, "OuterVision Power Supply Calculator" [Online]. Available: http://outervision.com/power-supply-calculator. [Accessed: 20-Oct-2016].

[34] Corsair, "PSU Finder" [Online]. Available: http://www.corsair.com/en-us/psu-finder. [Accessed: 20-Oct-2016].

[35] Ecova Plug Load Solutions, "80 PLUS Certified Power Supplies and Manufacturers" [Online]. Available: https://plugloadsolutions.com/80PlusPowerSupplies.aspx. [Accessed: 20-Oct-2016].

[36] Gabriel Torres, 2015, "Understanding the 80 Plus Certification - Page 3 of 4," Hardw. Secrets.

[37] newegg.com, "Thermaltake Toughpower Grand 1050W SLI/CrossFire Ready ATX 12V V2.3 / EPS 12V v2.92 80 PLUS GOLD Certified 7 Year Warranty Full Modular Active PFC Power Supply Haswell Ready PS-TPG-1050FPCGUS-1-Newegg.com" [Online]. Available: http://www.newegg.com/Product/Product.aspx?item=N82E16817153220. [Accessed: 21-Oct-2016].

[38] Wikipedia, the free encyclopedia, 2016, "Computer Fan," Wikipedia.

[39] Wikipedia, the free encyclopedia, 2015, "Active Cooling," Wikipedia.

[40] Wikipedia, the free encyclopedia, 2016, "Axial Fan Design," Wikipedia.

[41] Sam Pelonis, "Axial Vs. Centrifugal Fans" [Online]. Available: http://www.pelonistechnologies.com/blog/axial-vs.-centrifugal-fans. [Accessed: 21-Oct-2016].

[42] Wikipedia, the free encyclopedia, 2016, "Computer Fan Control," Wikipedia.

[43] Chris, "Air Flow VS. Static Pressure Fans – Choosing Between the Two - Superior Gaming Tech."

[44] noctua.at, "Which Fan Is Right for Me?" [Online]. Available: http://noctua.at/en/which_fan_is_right_for_me. [Accessed: 21-Oct-2016].

[45] Delta, "Delta Fan 120 X 120 X 38 MM SERIES" [Online]. Available: http://www.delta.com.tw/product/cp/dcfans/download/pdf/AFB/AFB120x120x38mm.pdf. [Accessed: 28-Jan-2017].

[46] Delta Electronics, "AFB 120x120x25.4mm Series" [Online]. Available: http://www.delta.com.tw/product/cp/dcfans/download/pdf/AFB/AFB120x120x25.4mm.pdf. [Accessed: 11-Mar-2017].

[47] Delta Electronics, "DC Brushless Fans & Blowers" [Online]. Available: http://www.delta.com.tw/product/cp/dcfans/dcfans_main.asp. [Accessed: 24-Feb-2017].

Chapter 3

Generated heat of a GPU mining rig and life span of components[1]

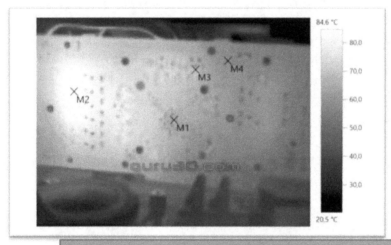

Thermal Imaging Measurements (FLIR) of MSI Radeon RX 470 Gaming X 8GB

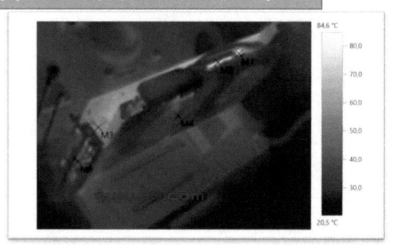

---

[1] Pictures were taken from guru3d.com, link is here!

3.1. How much heat does a GPU mining rig generate?

In this chapter, I am going to talk about generated heat from a mining rig and its effects on the lifespan of computer components. First, I am going to calculate how much heat a mining GPU generates, the calculations being done with a few examples of GPU mining rigs. Then, I will be talking about how the heat would affect the different components of the system. At the end, I have added a section on how to manage this heat and dissipate it effectively.

Computers use electric current to process information. Heat is dissipated in a computer component whenever the current flows [1]. Every computing device produces heat in proportion to the electricity it uses [2]. The main sources of heat generation in a desktop computer are, from highest to lowest, the GPU, CPU, PSU, mainboard VRM and mainboard chipsets. The amount of generated heat is directly related to the TDP design and architecture of the particular computer component.

Below, the heat generation in an example of an optimized 2017 Ethereum mining rig with four GPUs is shown. The mining rig consists of:

- Motherboard: Asrock B150A-X1 Intel 1151
- CPU: Intel Celeron G3900 2.8 GHz LGA1151 2 MB 51W TDP
- RAM: Crucial 8GB CL16 DDR4 DIMM Memory Module
- PSU: Corsair RM750x 80 PLUS Gold
- GPU: 4 pieces of AMD RX 480

Figure 1 - Picture of Corsair RM750x — 750 Watt 80 PLUS® Gold Certified Fully Modular PSU. It has 6+2 PCIE connectors which are adequate for six of AMD Radeon RX 470 GPUs.

Figure 2 - Picture of Asrock B150A-X1 motherboard. It has 5 available PCIE lanes.

Calculation:

- Motherboard + CPU + RAM: about 51 W + 10 W + 2 W for each 120-mm fan = 70 W[2]

- PSU: Corsair RM750x 80 PLUS Gold: 750 W by 10% = 75 W (90% is 80 Plus Gold efficiencies on 100% utilization [3])

- GPU: 4 units of AMD Radeon RX 480: 150 W TDP by 4 = 600 W

The system therefore generates almost 750 W of heat. This is about half of the heat that is produced by a typical hair dryer set at medium speed.

Now let's calculate the generated heat in another example. As you will see in Chapter 4 that I recommend the use of different GPU mining rigs with names of Ex02-1150-Rev01, Ex03-1150-Rev01, etc. where "Ex" stands for "Example", the second number indicates the number of GPUs, the number, 1150, refers to an Intel-1150 socket on the motherboard,

---

[2] The calculation of 70 watts is the maximum power consumption for the CPU, but the CPU remains mostly idle in an Ethereum mining rig while the mining work is done by the GPUs only.

and "Rev01" refers to the first version (updates may be required in the future). The details of these examples are given in the **Appendix** .

Here I calculate the heat generated by the **Ex05-1150-Rev01** system with five units of AMD Radeon RX 470 GPUs consisting of the following:

- Motherboard: Asrock H81 Pro BTC Motherboard
- CPU: Intel Celeron G1840
- RAM: HyperX 16 GB 1600 MHz CL9 DDR3
- PSU: Corsair RM1000x
- GPU: 5 units of PowerColor 4GB Red Devil RX 470
- Case Fan: 10 units of ARCTIC F12 PWM PST
- PCIE Riser: ELEGIANT USB 3.0 PCI-E Express 1x to 16x Extender
- Storage: SanDisk SSD Plus 120GB

Calculation:

- Motherboard + CPU + RAM: about 51 W + 10 W + 2 W for each 120-mm fan = 81 W
- PSU: Corsair RM750x 80 PLUS Gold = 750 W by 10% = 75 W (90% is 80 plus gold efficiencies on 100% utilization)
- GPU: 5 units of Radeon AMD RX 480: five times 120 W for the TDPs = 600 W

Thus, the system consumes = 600 + 75 + 81 = ~751 W. This value of 751 W is very close the maximum output of the Corsair RM750x PSU we chose, which is 750 watts. So choosing a more powerful PSU is recommended. Usually, the recommended wattage of a PSU for a GPU mining is equal to 110% of the consumption of the total system. For instance, if you calculate that the total consumption of the system is 500 watthours, it would be better to get a 110% of 500W, i.e. a PSU with 550 or more watts. In the previous system, a PSU with an output of 850–1000 W was recommended.

3.2. How does the heat affect your Ethereum mining rig?

3.2.1. Operating temperature and stability

The electronic components of any computer hardware are made of conductors such as gold, silver and copper, and semi-conductors such as silicon, germanium and selenium. The physical and chemical properties of these materials change as the temperature varies. For instance, the internal electrical resistance of copper increases by about 20% with a rise in temperature from 20° C to 100° C [4]. In addition, materials, in general, expand as the temperature increases. These changes may cause unwanted electrical interference and the components may not work as they are designed to. Consequently, an increase in temperature may make an electronic system unstable if it is not designed to withstand such an increase. This can be rectified either by designing the system to operate at the increased temperature, but this would make it much more expensive, or by cooling the components down to the desirable operating temperatures.

3.2.2. Life of components

The most common electronic component that is used in computers is capacitors—from the motherboard to the GPU. However, electrolytic capacitors are highly vulnerable to heat. Above the designed operating temperatures, constituents of the capacitors start to change their chemical and physical properties and deform, and the capacitors break down. The designed operating temperatures are usually mentioned on the product information paper. Ordinary aluminum electrolytic capacitors have an operating temperature of +85° C [5]; the new solid capacitors [6][3] which are commonly used in computer parts can be operated at up to +105° C. However, the estimated life of even these solid capacitors at this temperature is between 2000 and 5000 hours or about 200 days [7]. The table and chart below show the estimated lifespan of a solid capacitor at different operating temperatures.

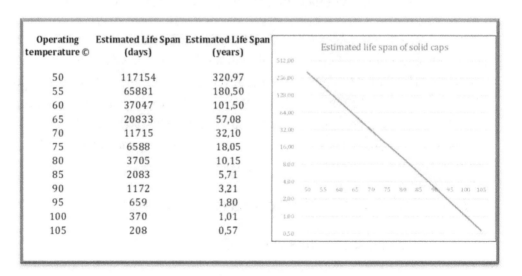

Operating temperature ©	Estimated Life Span (days)	Estimated Life Span (years)
50	117154	320,97
55	65881	180,50
60	37047	101,50
65	20833	57,08
70	11715	32,10
75	6588	18,05
80	3705	10,15
85	2083	5,71
90	1172	3,21
95	659	1,80
100	370	1,01
105	208	0,57

Estimated life span of solid caps

---

[3] In a solid electrolytic capacitor, the traditional liquid electrolyte is replaced by a solid conductive polymer electrolytic. This enhancement made the capacitor stronger against physical and thermal changes.

What happens in the real world situation? Why do some desktop computers last so long despite of not having a good cooling solution? The reasons are:

- A normal desktop computer doesn't work all the time; it may run few hours a day, perhaps for gaming or during working hours.
- A well-designed GPU, CPU or PSU has a cooling solution that keeps it cool even under heavy workload conditions so rarely the temperature exceeds 90° C—the cooling heatsinks and fans are designed to maintain an appropriate working temperature.
- The electronic components have safety measures so that when the temperature exceeds the design threshold, it shuts down to avoid being damaged.
- Even when you are gaming heavily, the GPU is not being utilized 100% of the time. There are moments when it runs under lower load and this helps the GPU to release some of the accumulated heat.

Why is heat management such a serious issue for an Ethereum mining rig?

The reason is that a mining rig operates 24/7 with 100% of the GPU's load. It costs a lot and needs to work uninterruptedly for a long time (at least 2 years until the next generation of GPUs are introduced). Also, as most Ethereum mining rigs are operated remotely (i.e. without direct supervision), stability of the system is much more important than is the case with a regular desktop computer.

As explained earlier, the maximum safe working temperature for a GPU is 80° C; above 80° C, the GPU becomes unstable for much of the time and usually throttles back. In addition, the life of the components will be lessened above this temperature.

3.3. How can I to manage the heat from GPUs and keep them cool enough?

GPUs are equipped with two designs of coolers or fans: 1. the blower-style or turbine; and 2. the open-air style. In the 1., the blower-type of cooler, there is a single centrifugal fan usually placed at the end of the card where usually the power connecters are placed. It sucks the air inside a fan shroud and blow it throw a heatsink which is usually connected to the GPU main chipset, VRMs and memory chips of the GPU. The warm air is then emitted from the GPU head where the output is placed. In the 2., the open-air design, there are multiple axial fans which blow air downwards to the designated heatsink which is connected to the GPU components, and the warmed air is exhausted to the surroundings, which is usually inside the computer case.

Most of the time, the open-air design has a superior heat transfer performance. The reasons are:

1. It has multiple fans that are larger than those of a single fan. Multiple fans have a higher potential to blow. An air blower must operate faster to move the same amount of air. Usually the blower-type fan is too noisy at high RPMs and multiple axial fans don't need to rotate at high speeds to transfer the same amount or more of air.
2. The blower-style design usually has a smaller heatsink due to the lack of space and this diminishes the performance of heat transfer. Open-air style coolers usually have large heatsinks equipped with multiple heat pipes to increase the heat-transfer rate.

Figure 3 - Picture of AMD Radeon RX 480 reference design, blower-style cooler

Figure 4 - Picture MSI AMD Radeon RX480 Gaming, with two axial fans, open-air style cooler

The only scenario in which a blower-style cooler shows a better performance than the other is in a relative small computer case, where it has been designed for micro ATX or mini ATX motherboards which do not have a proper inside airflow due to the lack of space. In this case, the GPU sucks air from outside and pushes it out through the exhaust slot. In a micro ATX case, usually only a single GPU can be installed, so a blower-style cooler is not a viable option for a professional mining rig.

Figure 5 - Picture of Xigmatek Octans Mini ITX Computer Case with Nvidia Reference design cooler.

Figure 6 - Picture of DAN Cases A4-SFX with a Nvidia GTX 780 Reference design GPU. Link to the DAN Cases is here! Arrows show the direction of incoming air and outgoing exhaust.

So, if the blower-style cooler performs worse than the other type, why do GPUs come with the original AMD Reference Designs or Nvidia Founders Edition from the factory?

The main reason is that it costs less! The design is simpler, requires no complex and sophisticated heatsink and heat-pipes, and uses only one intake fan. On the other hand, a simple blower-style cooler works fine for a desktop computer that doesn't undergo heavy or constant usage.

The graphic cards with a blower-centrifugal-style cooler and open-air-axial-type cooler are detailed in Chapter 2 and Chapter 5.

3.4. A small quiet mining rig is your best friend in the winter.

A small GPU mining rig, closed-air design[4] with two GPUs, and, for instance, with two AMD Radeon RX 480 4GB cards, consumes about ~400–500 W, on average. Imagine you work in a small room with a 10-square-meter area. I find the following rule-of-thumb to work well for non-insulated houses that are exposed to sunlight: in a living room, you will need 100 watts per square meter, i.e. 1,000 watts (1 kW) for a room of 10 m². In a bedroom, you will probably only need 75 watts per square meter: i.e. 750 watts for a room of 10 m². So, put simply, your small GPU mining rig can provide half of the required heating at the same time as it does the mining and make you some money. To understand more about the earnings and cost of such a small GPU mining rig, visit Chapters 4 and 5.

---

[4] In a closed-air design, the GPUs are placed in a closed compartment, such as a computer case, but in an open-air design, the GPUs are mounted on a chassis or a frame and are open to the outside. Please refer the part on chassis design in Chapter 5 to find out more on open-air and closed-air designs..

References

[1] Amollo, T. A., Kirui, M. S. K., Golicha, H. S. A., Kemei, S. K., and Nyakan, P. O., 2013, "Heat Dissipation in a Computer," Methods, **3**(6).

[2] smallbusiness.chron.com, "The Average Heat Output of a Computer" [Online]. Available: http://smallbusiness.chron.com/average-heat-output-computer-69494.html. [Accessed: 17-Oct-2016].

[3] Wikipedia, the free encyclopedia, 2016, "80 Plus," Wikipedia [Online]. Available: https://en.wikipedia.org/w/index.php?title=80_Plus&oldid=738657749. [Accessed: 17-Oct-2016].

[4] Temperature & Process Instruments, Inc., "Temperature vs Resistance Table of CU" [Online]. Available: http://www.tnp-instruments.com/sitebuildercontent/sitebuilderfiles/cu_100c_table.pdf. [Accessed: 18-Oct-2016].

[5] ILLINOIS CAPACITOR, "Aluminum Electrolytic Capacitors | Radial Lead | Axial Lead | Lytic | Low ESR | High Frequency" [Online]. Available: http://www.illinoiscapacitor.com/products/aluminum-electrolytic.aspx. [Accessed: 18-Oct-2016].

[6] Wikipedia, the free encyclopedia, 2016, "Polymer Capacitor," Wikipedia [Online]. Available: https://en.wikipedia.org/w/index.php?title=Polymer_capacitor&oldid=743974397. [Accessed: 18-Oct-2016].

[7] ASUS, "ASUS Motherboard - 78 Times Longer Lifespan than Expected!" [Online]. Available: http://event.asus.com/mb/5000hrs_VRM/. [Accessed: 18-Oct-2016].

Chapter 4

Let talk about money! Calculating the income, return on investment ...

4. Everything about income and money in short!

There are multiple factors that influence your earnings on an Ethereum Rig. These are:

1. The average hash rate of the system. Hash is a cryptographic function which takes an input (or 'message') and returns a fixed-size alphanumeric string, which is called the hash value [1]. At the moment, it is in megahashes (MH) on Ethereum systems. For instance, an AMD RX 470 makes 20-24 MH/s , and RX 570 24-28 MH/s on average.

2. The difficulty of the network[1]. In very general terms, this is the amount of effort required to mine a new block. This depends on the total hash rate of the network. In March 2017, the network difficulty was at 80 TH (tera hashes) [2].

$$more\ miners\ \rightarrow\ higher\ network\ difficulty$$
$$\rightarrow\ less\ total\ mined\ Ether\ per\ hash$$

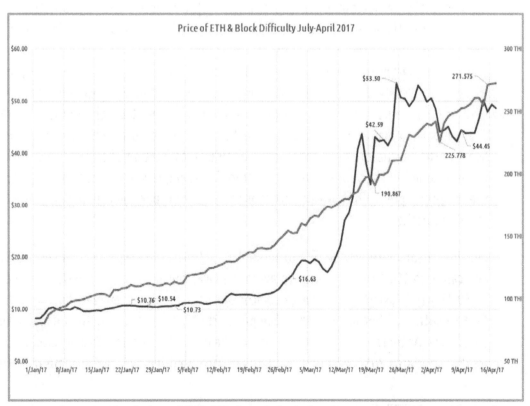

Figure 1 - Changes in price of Ether and Block difficulty at the beginning of 2017. As the price increased by 400% from $12 to 48$, many more miners came online and this movement resulted in increase of block difficulty.

---

[1] Block Difficulty is explained in Chapter 1.

3. The Ethereum Ether (ETH) price. A higher price of Ether (ETH) leads to increased earnings. At the moment, the price stays at about $8/ETH for Ether, and $1/ETC for Etherclassic [3] (please go to the link and check out the current prices. It varies a lot day during the day).

4. The average cost of electrical power. Usually, this stays at $0.1–$0.2 (€0.1–€0.2) per kWh. A cheaper power results in higher income.

5. Whether the mining rig is standalone or works in a shared mining pool. The income of non-pool miners depends on luck while a pool-miner has a steady income rate.

So how much can you make? After understanding the basics, now you need to use one of the many mining profit calculators that are available. Just search for "Ethereum or Ethereum classic mining calculator" on Google. What a profit calculator does is to give an income estimation at the end of the month based on the hash power of the GPU mining rig. The following links will take you to the websites with the calculators that I use personally—etherscan.io [4], and github.io [5]. On these sites, you can select your own sets of GPUs instead of entering the hash power[2]. The important points here are that as the time passes, 1. the network difficulty increases, and 2. the network hash power grows larger (the same number of distributed Ethers are split among many more miners), and therefore the Ether earnings will be lowered even though the Dollar earnings may remain the same or higher. If a miner makes 10 Ethers (~$100 if 1 ETH = $10) a month, it may make 7 Ethers (~$70 if 1 ETH = $10) a month by the end of the year. Some of the calculators have a feature to enable an estimation of the difficulty growth to be included in the year's profit prediction, for example see karldiab.com [6][3]. Avoid the long-term predictions of calculators as the price of Ether and the network difficulty are very volatile.

Consider a complete new system of mining rig, "Ex01-1150-Rev01", which costs €1589, and can hash 100–110 MH/s, with an average power consumption of 700 watts at a cost of $0.12 per kilowatt-hour. The calculator shows a projected income in 6 month of €236.42 with an Ether price of €8. If the price Ether increases to €10, the income would be €391.24. As there has been a giant leap in the price of Ether from $10 in January 2017 to ~$48 in March 2017, earnings would have increased but not at the same rate—the

---

[2] A GPU-mining calculator has three variable inputs, hash power of the rig and the power consumption of the rig and the price of electricity per kilowatt-hour. As I said, some profit calculators have the option of choosing GPUs instead of entering the hash power of the system directly, and the calculator estimates the hash power of a mining rig based on the recorded data.

[3] Attention: the calculation is based on the statistics as of that particular date. Always make your own calculations based on updated information from the websites using the links that I have provided. Please let me know if you find that one of the websites is no longer available.

earnings prediction shows a monthly profit of $1038!! But why didn't it grow by 4.5–4.8 times? This is because the network difficulty has also ballooned—to 197.575 TH (almost double that in January 2017); the highest average hashrate of 13093.3706 GH/s was recorded on Thursday, March 16, 2017. Thus, the important factors in this calculation are: 1. the price of hardware and electricity, 2. the block difficulty, and 3. the overall performance of the system. These are predictable or change only slightly in a 6–12 month period. But the price of Ether or Etherclassic varies a lot and rapidly—it can drop or increase by 20% in a few months, and therefore the predicted income can change. At the beginning of 2017 (i.e. based on the above figures), a rough calculation of the predicted income generated by a mining rig in 6 month is given by (€236.42 to €391.24)/(€1589), which is 14% to 24% of the total cost of the system. In a year, the predicted income would be 25% to 40%[4] of the total cost of the system if the total cost is taken to be €1589.

4.1. Costs and requirements of a GPU mining system

I have spoken about the predicted generating income of a mining rig in periods of 6 and 12 months. But, what about the 2nd and 3rd years of operation? And, how does a GPU mining system work on a large scale? The following factors need to be taken into the account:

1. The total cost of a GPU mining system.

2. The deprecation and loss of value of the system in the long-term, for example, over an expected life cycle of a GPU of 2 to 3 years.

3. The required space for a mining rig and for a mining system with more than 5 GPUs.

4. The maintenance, warranty, monitoring and breakdown costs and the costs of the required redundant components. The redundant components of a GPU mining rig(s) are the power supply, motherboard, physical drivers (SSDs) with the installed operating system, GPUs, etc.

5.   The costs and risks of total system breakdown, power cuts and other internet access disruptions, in short, anything that disturbs the mining process.

---

[4] The yearly income prediction is not proportional to what is made during a 6-month period. The income prediction rate declines as the time passes because of the increased network difficulty and growth in network mining power. For instance, if we make an income of 24% of the total system cost (as we calculated) in a 6-month period, this doesn't mean that we will make 48% in a 12-month period; the realistic rate would be about 40%.

4.3.1. Total cost of a GPU mining system

The major cost of a GPU mining rig is the cost of the GPUs themselves. The optimum number of GPUs per motherboard is 5. In the example system of Ex01-1150-Rev01 with 5 of AMD RX470 4GB, the total cost of the mining rig is €1589, while the cost of the GPUs is €1075 or 67.7% of the total cost. The formula below gives an approximate cost of a mining system with **NG** number of GPUs.

*Revised minercost is given by **NG** x Cost of GPU x 1.3*

For example, a miner system (consisting of many mining rigs) with 100 units of AMD Radeon RX470 4GB, costs: 100 x $215 x 1.3 = $27950

4.3.2. Depreciation of a mining a rig

As everyone knows, electronic equipment, especially computers, suffer from losing value for two reasons: 1. the normal depreciation process; and 2. the fact that newer items are continually being made available. I remember in the mid-90s, when I was in high school, the price of a $1000 computer was more than double the regular monthly salary of a worker; now it is a half of that. When the AMD Radeon RX 470 4GB was introduced in August 2016, I bought it for €250; now it would cost about €200, and the price may reduce even more during 2017, perhaps by another 20%. In addition, in the used marketplace, you may well find a AMD Radeon RX 470 4GB for about €150–170.

Another major factor affecting the depreciation of the value of computer components is the introduction of a new generation of a component. Now let's talk about depreciation on a GPU mining rig and its major components. GPU mining rigs mostly have **AMD** GPUs and Intel CPUs, and Intel CPU-compatible motherboards[5], but as said earlier, in a GPU mining rig we are not looking for a powerful CPU as the CPU stays idle most of the time. Also, the choice of motherboard is dependent of the number of available PCIE slots and other features of a motherboard are not important. Consequently, in a GPU mining rig, the motherboard, RAM and PSU manufacturers aren't so significant as long as the components provide the service expected of them. Currently Nvidia GPUs, at their current price and mining power are not efficient, specifically for mining Ethereum. So, I do not consider them further here.

---

[5] It has been explained in Chapter 2, and also in Chapter 5, any CPU requires a compatible motherboard socket and compatible motherboard chipset.

As discussed earlier in the topic of GPU-heat generation, I spoke about the linking of the GPU-manufacturing process and chipset size to the thermal design power (TDP) and heat-generation of a GPU. At the moment, AMD uses Polaris GPUs, which has the new 14-nm FinFET manufacturing process [7] which was introduced in June 2016 into the market. The next generation of chipsets with 10 nm or smaller, won't be expected to enter to the market before the end of 2017 or the beginning of 2018 [8]. Now consider, for example, the following case. Imagine that you build a GPU mining rig using "Ex05-1150-Rev01" system with a cost of €1589. After two years of operation, at some time during the summer of 2017, AMD introduces Radeon RX 570 8 GB at a price of €215 with a TDP of 120 watts with 10-nm process and the new GPU has with a 20% higher number of teraflops[6]. There are two obvious options that you could take:

1. Retire your system and buy the new, more powerful and efficient components; or

2. Continue using your 2-year-old system.

If you choose to go with **first option**, usually you don't have to rebuild or renew all your components. The CPU, motherboard, RAM, PSU and fans would work just fine and you will not have compatibility issues with the new GPUs, because there is no upcoming update until 2019 on the PCIE slot and other expansions that relate to GPU mining rigs. However, you will need to buy 5 new GPUs and get rid of your 5 AMD Radeon RX470 4GBs. You may use them as backup, build other systems with them or sell them. If you have decided to **sell** them, there are things you need to take into consideration:

1. A used mining GPU does not sell as well as a GPU that was used in a gaming desktop. This is because it has been used with a continuous 100% load, and therefore the expected life of the components would be lower compared to that of a GPU that has only been used for casual gaming or light desktop workloads.

2. The life expectancy of a GPU will be reduced when it operates at high temperature. As discussed in chapter 3, when a GPU runs at 90° C or higher all of the time, the GPU life expectancy may be reduced to about 3 years, while at 80° C, it could last for 18 years! When you sell a GPU that has worked under a mining load at high temperature, as a responsible and honest seller, you should inform the buyer of the card conditions under which the system has operated. In this book, I have already discussed how your mining rig with AMD Radeon RX470 and

---

[6] Flops are computation power, read more in Chapter 2.

RX480 cards could be made to operate below 80° C under all conditions, in order to extend the life of the components.

3. How much could your card be sold for after 2–3 years? Let's look at the R9 390 scenario. The last generation of AMD GPUs, at launch in the July of 2015, cost around $350 [9]; now it can be found for around $280–$310, an almost 20% price reduction. With a depreciation of around 20–30%, which is usually the case for electronic equipment the overall value of your system, if you had bought it in the summer of 2015 would have reduced by 40–50%. So, the current value would be around €215. By the end of 2018, it would sell for about €120–130.

Similarly, the value of the other components of system would also depreciate, but probably by not as much as the new GPU because: 1. they aren't top of the range components, and 2. they haven't been subjected to heavy loads like GPUs. Also, items such as the mining case and chassis, fans, etc. don't have much resale value in small quantities. My educated rough estimation of the overall depreciation in value of these components is 30% after the first year, 40% after 2 years and 50% at the end of the 3rd year. The deprecation is relative to how fast the next generation GPUs of AMD and Nvidia enter the market. At the moment, each year we see many new products which are more efficient and effective than the previous generation. Therefore their price falls off even more.

4.3.3. Required space for mining purposes

In addition to a space required for the actual mining rig(s), space is also necessary because the mining rig produces a lot of noise and heat and it needs to be able to work uninterruptedly.

1. Noise problem

My one year of experience with a GPU mining system is that "they are loud!". A mining GPU under 100% load always runs hot and therefore the GPU fan works continuously at high speed. If the setting of the fan of the GPU[7] remains untouched and the fan runs with its original factory settings, the GPU core clock frequency throttles back at a defined temperature, for example at 85° C or 90° C,

---

[7] There are many types of GPU customizing software available that let the professional user change the default setting of a GPU and customize it. For instance, the core GPU clock and memory frequency can be overclocked to run at higher rates. Also, the behavior of the fan of the GPU can be changed according to the GPU core temperature, and the speed with which a fan rotates can be programmed according to a new chart which is called "the fan curve". For instance, if originally the fan of a GPU rotates at 50% of its maximum at 80° C, it can be changed to rotate at 75% of its maximum. "MSI Afterburner " is an example of this software.

and the GPU runs at 800 megahertz instead of 1100 megahertz. Rarely, the GPU fan ramps up rapidly to 100%. In most GPUs that I have owned, the GPU fans are very loud when they run above 60% of their maximum speed. The loudness will depend on the number of GPU fans plus that of any extra 120-mm fans that you may have placed in the chassis and the PSU fan. Usually the noise of a mining rig with more than 5 GPUs is unbearable in the long-term. Consequently, GPU mining rigs require an isolated dedicated place or room like a computer-server room, where it is not bothered by other activities and doesn't bother people. Obviously, in a professional mining farm which is located in a warehouse or industrial place, noise is not a problem. Read more about this at the end of Chapter 5.

I personally have tried to suppress some of the noise with rubber acoustic foam or insulation foam. This helped but it is not effective if the fan outlets are open to the outside. You may design a noise blocking chassis to cover outlets of the sound wave. You can search on google for "noise cancelling computer case" to obtain some ideas on noise cancellation methods. These have been implemented in many computer cases such as Cooler Master Silencio 652S [10] or ST-860 from Silentmaxx [11].

2. Heat problem

In chapter 3, heat generation of a GPU mining system has been discussed. All of the electricity you put into the system converts to heat. For example, the Ex01-1150-Rev01 mining rig produces up to 1000 watts of heat. If the designated room has no active cooling system, the temperature of system will eventually rise and therefore the temperature of the running GPUs would increase. A GPU mining system cannot be operated efficiently in a small area without active cooling. My suggestion is that, in winter, when possible, the generated heat of the GPU mining rig should be used to heat the inside environment. In summer and on hot days however, the heat will need to be dispersed outside.

How hot does the air get? My temperature reading of the exhaust air from a well-ventilated closed case of a mining rig never exceeds 55° C while the GPUs' core is running at 70°–80° C with an ambient temperature of 21°–23° C degrees. When many mining rigs operate in a facility, there may a way to use this warm exhaust air, perhaps to heat up a boiler, but recycling the hot air that comes out of a computer room requires careful planning and this makes the whole system much more complicated and expensive, sometimes many times more than the total cost of the whole mining system. So, as I mentioned earlier, the simple and practical solution is to route the warm air into the building itself with simple air channels or ducts when it is necessary and desirable.

The space required for a multiple mining rig is as follows:

1. A minimum of 1 square meter per mining rig with five GPUs.

2. An air intake duct, window or channel that 1. filters the dust out, and 2. controls the humidity.

3. Air intake suction fans or blowers.

4. An air exhaust duct, window or channel.

5. An exhaust fan or blower[8].

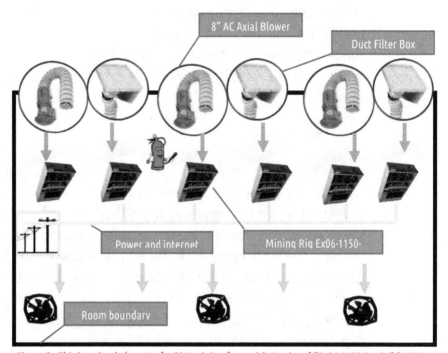

Figure 2 - This is a simple layout of a GPU-mining farm with 6 units of "Ex06-1150-Rev01" (6 GPUs mining rig, link to the duct filter and axial fan are here!)

In many ventilation systems, for instance in most restaurants, there are only exhaust fans and the intake air enters naturally. Such exhaust fans create a negative pressure inside the environment and this forces air to enter to the room or building. My recommendation would be to use an exhaust system because the generated heat in

---

[8] Read more about building a GPU miner in Chapter 5 and 6.

the room must be removed, particularly in hot weather. Of course, if an exhaust system is used, there will need to be a clear route for the air intake to enter. A system that has a good forced-air exhaust system, does not require intake fans as well. In a dusty and polluted environment, an intake air filter is necessary to lower the risk of dust buildup on the computer fans that may eventually interrupt the operation of the system. The dust filter lowers the time and cost of maintenance in the long run.

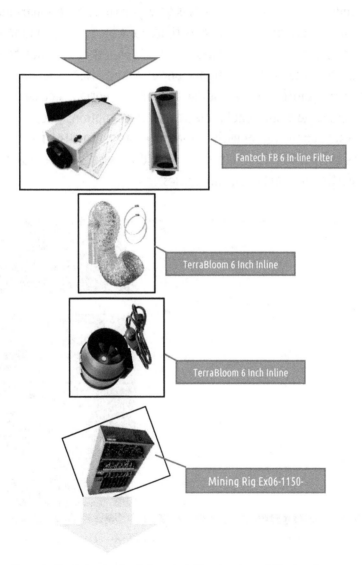

Figure 3 - Simple layout of an inline 6-inch filtration channel. The brands here are not given as recommendations; just as examples.

4.3.4. Power and internet connection

Each GPU mining rig requires a separate protected power connection that is able to deliver up to 1200 watts for a 5-GPU mining rig (if you use some old power-hungry cards like AMD R9 Fury, you will need 1500 watts). Usually the maximum deliverable power in a household is around 13–20 amps for a 220–230 V system. This makes it suitable for the supply of up to about 3000 watts (more or less) of electricity continuously. For mining purposes only, you could have a maximum of twenty GPUs running in such place at the same time. For a bigger system than that, you will need an industrial perhaps 3-phase power connection or business type of power connection that offers a higher power supply. Note that in some countries, the electricity tariff is on a sliding scale for a normal household, and in order to encourage low household electricity consumption, the cost of electricity per kilowatt-hour increases with increasing consumption. So, if you are planning to have more than a 6-GPU mining rig, it would be wise to apply for an upgraded power connection to avoid these difficulties.

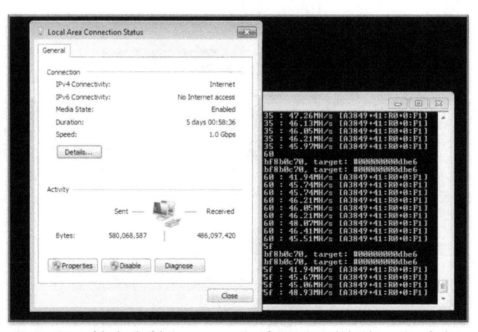

Figure 4 - Picture of the details of the internet connection of a test-miner, which with an uptime of 5 days, sent almost 480 MB and downloaded 553 MB.

For a GPU mining rig, you will require an internet connection which stays connected to the network all the time, especially if you do pool mining. The speed and bandwidth are not important. You do not even require a large internet package and the internet connection can be broadband, mobile or landline. The maximum download is limited, and in most of cases a 10 GB data plan is more than enough.

One of my systems with three GPUs, that has an uptime of 5 days, downloaded almost 500 megabytes and sent 480 megabytes. So, in a month, you will require to be able to transfer about 3–5 GB of data. The most important aspect of an internet service is its stability of connection as you will need to stay connected all the time.

Figure 5 - Picture of ASUS RT-AC51U wireless router with a 4G USB modem

4.2. Return on investment, long-term thinking!

Here I'm going to do an analysis of where we might be at the end of the 2nd and 3rd years with a GPU mining system—to determine whether or not it is worth doing.

The calculation is in U.S. Dollars, although as of the time of writing, the Euro and U.S. Dollar are very close. In these calculation, I assume near perfect conditions, i.e., a place with no disruption, the internet and power supply always running perfectly, no breakdowns, etc. Later on, I will take account of the risks of failure of the system in order to get closer to the real-world situation.

The installation and operational costs on the balance sheet are:

1. Five GPUs in a mining rig of Ex05-1150-Rev01 = 5 x $1589 = $7945.
2. Renting a 20-square-meter room = $200 per month = $2400/year.
3. Internet = $20 per month, $240/year.
4. Ventilation system = 5% of the cost of the mining system (this is for a simple system!) = $400.
5. Power cost calculated with the Ethereum profit calculator = $2629.8/year.
6. Depreciation value of the system by the end of 3rd year = 40% ($7945) = $3178.

Motherboard	ASRock H81 Pro BTC Motherboard	€75.00		1	€75.00
CPU	Intel Celeron G1840	€36.00		1	€36.00
RAM	HyperX 16 GB 1600 Mhz CL9 DDR3	€60.00		1	€60.00
PSU	Corsair RM1000x	€170.00		1	€170.00
GPU	PowerColor 4gb Red Devil RX 470	€215.00		5	€1,075.00
Case Fan	ARCTIC F12 PWM PST	€6.00		8	€48.00
PCIE Riser	ELEGIANT USB 3.0 PCI-E Express 1x to 16x Extender	€10.00		4	€40.00
Storage	SanDisk SSD Plus 120GB	€45.00		1	€45.00
OS	Windows 7 OEM	€25.00		1	€25.00
Chasis	Used wooden cabinet	€15.00		1	€15.00
			Total =		€1,589.00
			GPU cost/Total =		68%
			(Mobo + CPU + Ram) / Total =		11%

The profit value is only the profit made by a GPU miner, generating Ether (ETH) or Classicether (ETC).

This is very tricky. According to the calculations of karldiab.com, with the current network difficulty[9] growth and maximum hash power of the entire network, the mining system will not make a profit until after the **14th month of operation**, with the current price of Ether at $8 and the price of electricity of $0.1/kWh. Most Ethereum calculators and formulas don't take price changes, network difficulty growth, and increased number of hash power into the account. My educated guess is that the price of Ether will eventually increase as the network difficulty and size of the blockchain grows, but by how much, I don't know! Is it worth spending thousands or millions of Dollars on it? I'd say this is risky. GPU mining systems are so new and things change every month, but does it have a bright future? Certainly, it has.

I will base my profit prediction on a middle-ground scenario. I assume that the price of Ether would increase with network difficulty, so I will calculate the safe income in one year with dynamic growth and multiply it by 3 years, assuming that in the second and third years the system will produce the same profit range.

Without dynamic difficulty, Ether at $8, cost of power at $0.12/kWh, a 500 MH/s rig and consuming 3000 watts of electricity, would make $4400–$5100 in one year.

With a difficulty of 82 trillion now and dynamic difficulty, and a growth rate of 11 trillion/month, earning of a 500 MH/s rig would be $1815 in one year.

---

[9] As said earlier, please read more on network difficulty and hashing power of network in Chapter 1.

With a growth rate of 5 trillion/month, it would be $2846 in one year.

But block difficulty does not have a stable pattern yet! As you can see in the history chat over many months, it even has negative values!

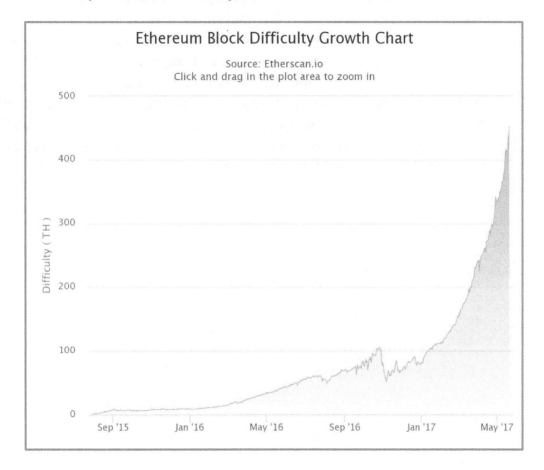

So, what we are going to do? As the price of Ether became mature, and many miners took Ethereum seriously as they did Bitcoin mining, I started to invest in it in April 2016. I will therefore make a new chart from April 2016, compare it with the price of Ethereum, and leverage the difficulty growth and make a prediction for the first year of operation.

First, we have the **Earning Ratio chart**, which is calculated by dividing the price of Ether in USD by the difficulty. Higher numbers result in higher expected earnings. If Ether (ETH) is sold within the same price range, as we calculated for the earnings, while it is possible to mine Ether or Ether Classic and not sell immediately, you have the option of saving it in your wallet and selling it later when the price is better. However, this makes the calculation a little more complicated as you might need to calculate the interest that would have been obtained by selling your Ether immediately and putting the money into an account that gains interest.[10] How? I will explain in a hypothetical scenario. Imagine your GPU mining rig is making 1 Ether a day with a network difficulty of 100 TH. By the end of the year, as more miners come online and join the network (i.e. there would have been an increase in hashing power), and as network difficulty increases, your Ether earning would decrease to 0.5 ETH a day. However, you have the option of saving all of the earned Ethers during the year and selling them when the price is good for you. Any unspent Ether in your Ether wallet[11]— say, for example, you had collected 270 Ether (ETH) in the whole year—may give you a small interest, if you had it sold the Ether immediately after you had earned it and invested it. For instance, if you sell your daily 1 Ether and save the money in a bank, you might get 5% yearly interest on it. This would have to be included in your financial calculations. This interest may seem small for a single GPU mining rig, but not for a million-dollar mining farm.

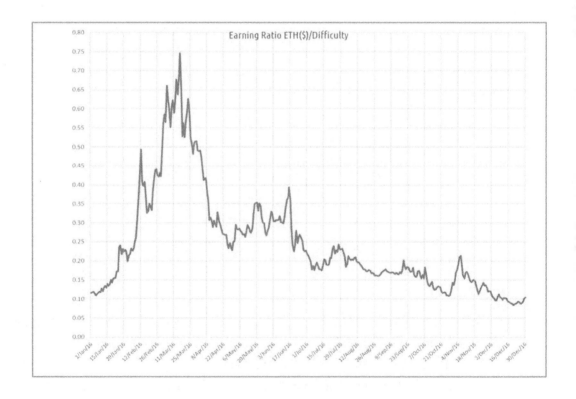

---

[10] The work sheets for all of the charts can be found in the attachment and appendix section of this book.
[11] Wallet is explained in Chapter 1.

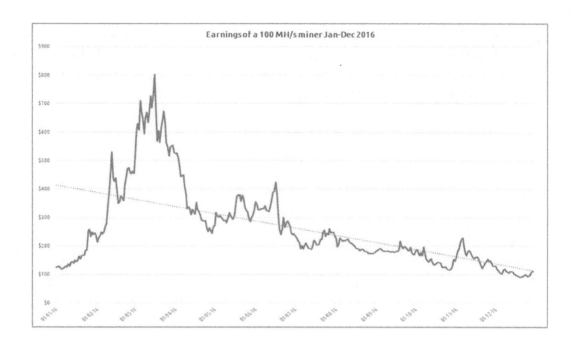

These two charts show the estimated monthly earnings of a 100 MH/s GPU miner. The chart above shows the whole period of 2016, as the price of Ether and network difficulty were volatile and therefore earnings fluctuated a lot. At the end of December 2016, the earnings prediction was $112 per month for a 100 MH/s mining rig, excluding the costs of power.

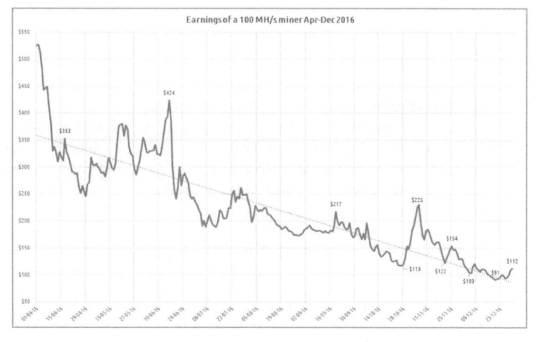

During the April to December period in 2016, the Ether price became stable and the earnings of a 100 MH/s miner became steadier and followed a pattern.

From these figures, we can see that the general decrease in earnings that occurred since the beginning of the existence of the Ethereum network as the network difficulty became more complex and more miners come online but only the same amount of Ether[12] is available to be distributed to miners.

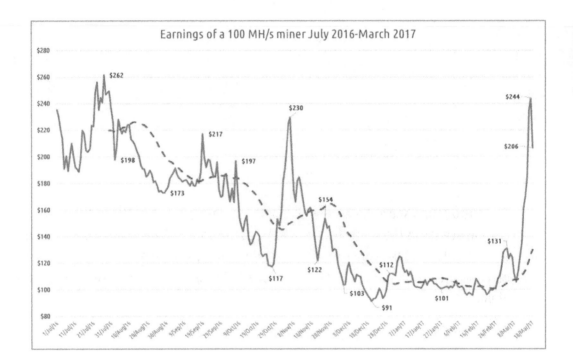

The redline shows the average earnings movement from July 2016 until March 2017. As said earlier, at the end of February 2017, the price of Ether jumped by 400%! and surprised everyone. All of the price predictions, earnings calculations and estimated returns on investment needed to be reevaluated. The price of ~$48 is not expected to remain steady for long—the price increase was due to the total number of miners and network difficulty having doubled.

Let's get back to the balance sheet again. The total costs by the end of the 3rd year would be:

- 5 mining rigs of Ex05-1150-Rev01 = 5 x $1589 = $7945.

---

[12] As we read in Chapter 1, at the moment 18 million Ether are being distributed yearly.

- Renting a 20-square-meter room = $2400/year x 3 = $7200.

- Internet = $20 per month, $240/year x 3 = $720.

- Ventilation system = 5% of mining system (a simple system design) = $400.

- Power cost = $2629.8/year x 3 = $7889.4 (this should be deducted from earnings).

- Depreciation value of the system at the end of 3rd year = 40% ($7945) = $3178.

Total = $19443 (power cost deducted in the Ether profit calculator)

Your earnings?

- Without dynamic difficulty, the maximum would be $15,000.

- With difficulty growth and earnings reducing by 5% per month, the earning would be $2846 x 3, i.e. $8,538.

So, the profit is negative. Sad and disappointed? Me too! Why did it happen? There are several reasons:

1. A major cost is the rent of the place at an average of $200 per month. This needs to be lowered or eliminated altogether. How can this be done? A mining-rig room doesn't have to be sophisticated or close to the city. It can be located anywhere as long as the requirements of a mining rig are satisfied (I have explained them earlier) and system works uninterruptedly and is stable. A storage room or unwanted extra space works well. The total cost without the room rent is $19443 - $7200 = $12243

2. At the beginning of 2017, Ether was around the **unfair[13] price of $8** due mainly to recent platform difficulties in the algorithm, network hacks, chain fork and changes to the process (more can be read about this online). The fair price in my opinion is around $12, i.e. 50% more. If the price were $12, our predicated earnings would be 150% of $8538 (i.e. $12807).

---

[13] Why did I call it unfair? In a healthy mature demand and supply system, when you have a limited supply and your demand is increasing every day, the value or price of the product or service increases to maintain the balance. In the Ether (ETH) case, some minor technical difficulties with the platform resulted in distrust in the network and unpopularity, and the price of Ether(ETH) crashed by 50% from $12 to $8 between November 2016 and January 2017.

If you can manage the cost of renting a place somehow, by the end of the 3rd year, you should be able to balance the total cost of your system.

This is just a simple example of how a system might work. I'm not an accountant or financial expert who can take everything into account but I have tried to show you a way to calculate your own costs and predict your earnings and therefore profit by the end of a particular period.

Anyhow, as the price of Ether broke its record in the middle of March 2017, I'm going to calculate the whole thing again with the new price.

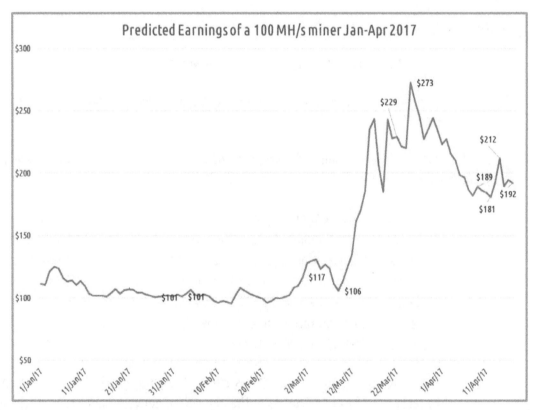

Figure 6 - Picture shows a jump on earnings of an Ethereum-GPU miner due to an increase of price from $12 to over $50.

Similar to the previous balance sheet calculation with 1 Ether = $8, the cost and negative values are almost the same, it's just that there was a decrease on the price of GPUs, according to mid-April prices:

The installation and operational costs at the end of 3rd year mining are:

1. Five GPUs in a mining rig of Ex06-1150-Rev02 = 5 x €1,758 = €8,790 or $8,790.

*Table 2 - Specification of **Ex06-1150-Rev02** GPU-mining rig with updated prices of mid-April 2017*

Motherboard	ASRock H81 Pro BTC Motherboard	€75.00	1	€75.00
CPU	Intel Celeron G1840	€36.00	1	€36.00
RAM	HyperX 8 GB 1600 Mhz CL9 DDR3	€35.00	1	€35.00
PSU	Corsair RM1000x	€165.00	1	€165.00
GPU	Gigabyte RX470 G1 Gaming 4GB	€195.00	6	€1,170.00
Case Fan	ARCTIC F12 PWM PST	€6.00	12	€72.00
PCIE Riser	ELEGIANT USB 3.0 PCI-E Express 1x to 16x Extender	€10.00	6	€60.00
Storage	SanDisk SSD Plus 120GB	€45.00	1	€45.00
OS	Linux UBUNTU 16.04	€0.00	1	€0.00
Chasis	Proper Mining Chassis	€100.00	1	€100.00
		Total =		**€1,758.00**
		GPU cost/Total =		**67%**
		(Mobo + CPU + Ram) / Total =		**8%**

2. Renting a 20-square-meter room = $2400/year x 3 = $7200.
3. Internet = $20 per month, $240/year x 3 = $720.
4. Ventilation system = 5% of the cost of the mining system (this is for a simple system) = $400.
5. Power cost = $3,628/year x 3 = $10,886 (this will be deducted from earnings).
6. Depreciation value of the system by the end of 3rd year = 40% ($8,790) = $3,516.

Total cost = $20,626 (power cost deducted in the Ether profit calculator)

The Earnings:

The profit (earnings minus power cost) made by five units of a Ex06-1150-Rev02 GPU-miner with the following parameters:

1. Price of Ether (ETH) of $48.83,
2. Cost of power of $0.12/kWh,
3. Hash rate of 640 MH/s (5 X 128 MH/s),
4. Power consumption of 3500 watts, and
5. Block difficulty of 277.5351 TH, increasing by 87.95 TH per month,

would be ~$1,049 in the first month, about ~$3,158 in the first six months and about $4,500–$5,500 in a year.

Thus, the profit from this small GPU mining farm by the end of the 3rd year is negative despite the 400% increase in the price of Ether from $12 in January 2017 to over $50 in April 2017. As said earlier, the main reason for this is the cost of the rent of a place which is $7,200.

Since March of 2017 until June of 2017, the price of Ether (ETH) has gone nuts. It has increase from ~$50 to ~ $190, almost four times. On the other hand, the network hash rate has increase from 16508 GH/s on 30th of March to 29819.2767 GH/s in 25th May 2017, the increase of less than 200%. The Block difficulty of 236.982 TH increased to 463.103 TH in the same period. As a result, the earning and profit has increased dramatically.

Calculation of profit per month of a six GPU mining rig of Ex06-1150-Rev02, with 160 MH/s, with power draw of 850 W is $856.52, where is $91.80 has been deducted as power cost. Mining metrics are calculated based on a network hash rate of 29,821 GH/s and using a ETH - USD exchange rate of 1 ETH = $ 204.53. These figures vary based on the total network hash rate and on the ETH to USD conversion rate. Block reward is fixed at 5 ETH and future block reward reductions are not taken into account. The average block time used in the calculation is 15 seconds. The electricity price used in generating these metrics is $ 0.15 per kWh.

Although this earning and high profit are not going to continue for a long, but they stir up all of the previous calculations which I have done. This high profit will attract attentions of so many more people and their investment into the GPU mining business, consequently block difficulty and network hash power will increase, and it most probably will diminish the profits, if Ether stays in the same price. However, these are all speculations, nothing is certain and last for a long in this business. Finally, it looks so promising and worth investing but you may take extra caution as these numbers aren't stable and may turn down so quickly.

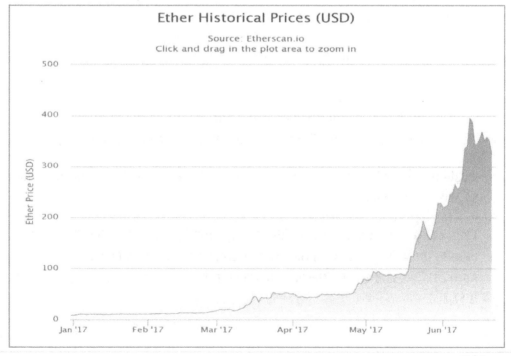

Based on the end of June 2017 calculation, profit per month is $ 786.60, where this rig can mine 2.67 ETH per month, with mining metrics which are calculated based on a network hash rate of 51,857 GH/s and using a ETH - USD exchange rate of 1 ETH = $ 324.24. The electricity price used in generating these metrics is $ 0.12 per kWh.

All of these calculations here are just some examples to teach you how to do yours, so do not rely on the numbers that I have brought here, while they most probably would be outdated at the time you are reading this book. What you need to do is learn the method, calculate the cost of your system based on the up-to-dated price market, then come to the balance sheet and apply them with assistant of a profit calculator. Again, I need to mention that the profit declines as the time passes, while the network hash power and block difficulty increases. The only factor that kept the profit of GPU mining rig and mining cryptocurrency so high is the increase on price of that particular cryptocurrency that you mine. The moment that the price of cryptocurrency stops to incline or decrease, the earning and therefore the profit would lessen.

4.3.Maintenance, warranty, monitoring, breakdown, power shortage, etc.

At the beginning of this chapter, I mentioned that no business or operation works without problems and risks. Based on my one year of mining experience, I am sure that you will experience a lot of breakdowns in your mining system. A mining rig would crash and freeze for many reasons, one being that the main purpose of the components is not GPU mining. In a mining-rig computer, the stability of the system is not comparable to a server computer that runs for a long time without interruption. What are the differences?

1. A server computer is designed to work at a steady rate; it has dual, quad or more CPUs per system. This provides a higher performance and lower stress than a single CPU unit.
2. The RAM modules of a server computer are ECC (with error correction) and buffered to avoid data corruptions and increase stability.
3. Server computers generally use redundant power supplies in pairs, so that when one fails the other one supplies power to the system.
4. Storage units usually work in pairs in a Raid system, Raid 1, 5, 10, etc., and usually they have backup storage in case of major failures.
5. Server units have exceptionally good cooling systems and usually are very loud.
6. Many server computers are equipped with UPS and a backup battery to power up the system until any interruption is resolved or the ongoing operations are saved and stored safely.
7. A server computer uses a special operation system such as Windows Server or Linux Server editions. Such an OS offers a lot more stability and inside control features.

In a regular mining rig, we don't implement any of these not because it is not possible but because they would make the mining rig too expensive and it would not be feasible to make money from it. In addition, the mining programs are at early stages of development. Many of them are not stable enough and this causes the system to crash and freeze. Also, GPU mining is dependent on the AMD GPU drivers. No GPU-driver software is made for GPU mining; therefore, they may react very oddly at times. I have seen incidents in which the GPU fan ramps up so rapidly or gets stuck at maximum speed and the problem could not be fixed by the AMD Crimson software[14] and I had to restart the whole unit. Most of the time, temperature monitoring and frequency modification

---

[14] AMD Crimson software is the genuine default software developed by AMD that contains driver and setup software for AMD GPUs. An AMD GPU works properly in an operation system when Crimson is installed.

are hard to achieve and you will require additional software such as MSI afterburner. Mining rigs usually use Windows 7 or Linux systems such as Ubuntu, Mint, Fedora, etc. Again, as said earlier, these operational systems are not optimized to run 24/7 in high-stress and hot-environment GPU mining computers.

Also, any computer component can breakdown and shutdown the computer. The most vulnerable components in a miner are the GPUs and power supply that always work at near maximum capacities. It is a good idea if you spend 5% of your total budget on redundant or reserve components. When a GPU breaks down, it can simply be taken out of the system—the system would still be operational without one of its GPUs, although it would produce less hash power for mining. But when a power supply breaks down, the whole system shuts off and quick replacement is crucial. So, even when your budget is tight, try to use a reliable power supply, and if you have multiple mining rigs, you should keep one extra PSU for rainy days. The CPU, motherboard and RAM do not operate under a heavy load in a GPU mining system and therefore the chance of a breakdown is minimal. Even so, as a GPU mining rig has multiple GPUs, it will work fine even if one of the GPUs breaks down, as usually a defective GPU does not interrupt the mining operation. The defective GPU can eventually be replaced.

4.3.1. Monitoring your mining rig remotely

A GPU mining rig can be remotely monitored in the same way as any desktop computer. I, personally, in Windows operation system and in Linux Ubuntu use TeamViewer[15] [12], the free version for personal use. There are many other programs available online, either paid or free versions. For instant SMOS is an Ubuntu based operation system which is customized only for GPU mining, it has very easy and effective remote control but it costs $2 per rig per month (read more about it on Chapter 5 and 6). You may update your mining software, batch files and other things, make changes, and restart the computer remotely. However, if you lose internet connection to the mining rig, for some reason or other, you won't be able to have access to the system anymore! Also, it happened to me on many occasions that changes to the system which I made remotely make it unstable; sometimes it crashed or froze and I needed to manually restart the system. Consequently, maintenance and monitoring issues and tasks are part of any computer running business and will eventually add up to the overhead cost of running the system.

4.3.2. Warranty issues

---

[15] Remember! Team Viewer free version is designated for personal use. If you are planning for a full-scale mining farm, commercial-use or to do it in any other way than experimenting, you should buy the commercial version.

The GPU doesn't die from the workload of mining and the generated heat faster than expected. Why?

1. As I explained in **Chapter 3 on** heat management, the electronic components do not die even in temperatures over 100° C.
2. Most of the components never reach above 90° C as they are protected by thermal safety measures—the card would freeze or crash before it starts being damaged.
3. By design, any GPU has active cooling that removes the heat from its main components, such as the GPU core, power delivery system and memory modules. So, these components never get too hot and always stay within the operating temperature.
4. In the GPU bios and also the AMD Crimson driver software, the maximum reachable temperature is limited, usually around 90°–95° C. The card will shut off or throttle the clock frequency down to reduce the generating heat.

Even with the default factory settings, GPUs in a mining rig would probably work for at least 3 years (with a 95% probability). In the case of unexpected events, the GPU card has a warranty that you may use to claim if something goes wrong. Usually manufacturers offer at least 2 years of limited warranty on normal cards, and offer extended warranties of 3 to 5 years on the top of the range cards. In a GPU mining rig, cooling fans are usually set to work 100% of the time, in order to provide the maximum airflow during the mining operation and keep the card as cool as possible.

XFX[16] covers a minimum of 2 years with normal cards, 3 years with RS cards and 5 years with premium GTR cards [13]. Often, the warranty terms and conditions or period of cover are not mentioned on the manufacturer's product page and also they vary from reseller to reseller, or country to country. It would be wise to email the manufacturer's representative, agent or reseller and ask about the period of warranty and what it covers before you purchase.

Usually premium cards are a little more expensive (around 20–30% more) but they have 1. premium components, 2. a higher TDP design with a stronger power delivery system, 3. a better cooling unit, with a larger heat sink, which most of the time comes with a back plate, and 4. a better warranty. So, it is not a bad idea to go for such an option, when it is possible.

---

[16] Here I need to admire the XFX, it is the only manufacturer that states the warranty period and condition openly and clearly in their website, I haven't found such information on any other manufacturers unless you send an email or attempt to buy the card and you have found the information in the last moment before you pay for the item.

Getting back to the original topic of costs and hassles of maintenance and warranty, if a GPU card fails and you have to claim under the warranty, you will have to deal with a downtime until you receive a new card or repaired one. This may take up to two months. In addition, you will usually have to pay for the shipping costs. In your analysis and risk management, you will need to consider an inevitable small downtime, for instance, 5% of the total mining time.

4.3.3. Maintenance costs of a mining rig

A mining rig does not work like your ordinary desktop computer. Apart from having the basic software and a minimal firewall or antivirus protection, you don't have to install anything further. Only occasionally, you may have to update the mining software if the update provides you with more useful features. The GPU-driver software does not require updates as your system works with a simple mining software.

As far as the hardware is concerned, the most important maintenance that needs to be carried out is removing the accumulated dust, when required. Sometimes, a GPU fan becomes noisy and starts to fail. But this won't be apparent on a remote system, so, on-site visits will be necessary to check that everything is working fine. Alternatively, the condition of the fans can be checked by adding a simple microphone to the system using remote monitoring software. If the system consists of many mining rigs, active monitoring is essential and the cost of this must be taken into the account.

References

[1]   Ethdocs.org, "Ethereum Homestead 0.1 Documentation" [Online]. Available: http://ethdocs.org/en/latest/glossary.html. [Accessed: 28-Dec-2016].

[2]   Etherscan, "Ethereum Block Difficulty Growth Chart" [Online]. Available: https://etherscan.io/chart/difficulty. [Accessed: 28-Dec-2016].

[3]   Etherscan, "Ethereum (Ether) Historical Prices" [Online]. Available: https://etherscan.io/chart/price. [Accessed: 28-Dec-2016].

[4]   Etherscan, "Ethereum Mining Profitablity Calculator" [Online]. Available: https://etherscan.io/ether-mining-calculator. [Accessed: 29-Dec-2016].

[5]   github.io, "Ethereum Mining Profitability Calculator" [Online]. Available: https://badmofo.github.io/ethereum-mining-calculator/. [Accessed: 29-Dec-2016].

[6]   karldiab.com, "Ethereum Mining Calculator" [Online]. Available: http://www.karldiab.com/EthereumMiningCalculator/. [Accessed: 29-Dec-2016].

[7]   Wikipedia, the free encyclopedia, 2016, "AMD Radeon 400 Series," Wikipedia.

[8]   Wikipedia, the free encyclopedia, 2016, "10 Nanometer," Wikipedia.

[9]   Smith, R., "AMD Launches Retail Radeon 300 Series: A Prelude To Fury" [Online]. Available: http://www.anandtech.com/show/9387/amd-radeon-300-series. [Accessed: 30-Dec-2016].

[10] Cooler Master, "Cooler Master: Silencio 652S" [Online]. Available: http://www.coolermaster.com/case/mid-tower-silent-series/silencio652s/. [Accessed: 30-Dec-2016].

[11] Silentmaxx, "Leise PC Gehäuse ST-860 Gedämmte Tower" [Online]. Available: http://www.silentmaxx.de/leise-komponenten/gedaemmter-tower-silentmaxxr-st-860.html. [Accessed: 30-Dec-2016].

[12] TeamViewer, "TeamViewer – Access Your Computer Remotely and Share Your Desktop with Friends – It's Free for Personal Use!" [Online]. Available: https://www.teamviewer.com/en/. [Accessed: 01-Jan-2017].

[13] XFX, "XFX Warranty" [Online]. Available: http://xfxforce.com/en-us/support/xfx-warranty. [Accessed: 02-Jan-2017].

Chapter 5

Configuration of a GPU mining rig[1]

Picture of a neat home-made GPU mining rig

---

[1] Here is the link of the source of pictures!

5. Building an Ethereum-mining rig

In this section, we will build a GPU mining rig together. I have focused on building an Ethereum-mining rig because at the moment Ethereum is the most promising GPU mining platform as it pays much better than the other cryptocurrencies that are available and there is therefore a better probability of getting a return on one's investment. After some setbacks with the Ethereum platform, Ethereum classic has recently gained momentum and now trades very well. In the first quarter of 2017, Ethereum-Classic (ETC) mining became very profitable as the price of ETC increased to $2.58[2] on April 10, 2017, whereas it was below $1[3] since 2nd November 2016. On March 30, 2017, one Ether has been traded for $52.98, while it was $10.47 on 30th January 2017. On May 2017, the Ethereum price has gone crazy, Ether (ETH) has soared up to over $200 on 25th May 2017 and Classic (ETH) has gone up to 1 ETC = $18.19. On 23th June 2017, Ethereum Classic network hash rate was 3,487 GH/s and 1 ETC trades $19.12 while Ethereum network hash rare was 51,876 GH/s at price of 1 ETH = $ 320.1.

If you already know a lot about Ethereum and GPU mining and have skipped Chapters 1 and 2, I recommend that you read Chapters 3 and 4 first, as those chapters give you a better idea about entering the GPU mining business. I have divided this chapter into sections based on the goals of the reader. Some readers may only want to try GPU mining for a while just to experiment. I, myself, was not sure about Ethereum when I started myself and so I let my system farm run for a while until I was able to cash some of my first Ethers. It was only after that that I started to become more involved in it. If you already have a desktop PC, you probably can start Ether mining right away. Only some small modifications may be required. There are thousands of articles, videos, etc. on the Internet that could help you with this. Here, I have tried to summarize everything for any newbie who wishes to make his/her mining rig.

If you want to know about individual mining-rig components, read Chapter 2. Most of the information in that chapter relates to general computer hardware, which I have considered from the viewpoint of a GPU mining rig. At the end of Chapter 2, there is an appendix which discusses some of the components of a mining rig, viz. PCIE-riser cards, cooling fans, mining chassis ideas, etc. You should know about these things before building a GPU mining rig.

---

[2] Please check the up-to-date price at website such as coinmarketcap.com The prices which are mentioned here are just examples.
[3] In this book, I assume that the US Dollar and Euro are numerically so close in value that I have used them interchangeably.

5.1. Design of a GPU-miner chassis

There are two distinct types of chassis design; an **open-air mining rig** and **closed-air mining rig**. Most of professional mining rigs are of the open-air design. Each design has advantages and disadvantages.

5.1.1. Open-air design

Here, I have collected many of the different types of open-air designs that I found on the Internet (the references are given so that you can do your own research, if necessary) and I added have my own comments and suggestions.

An open-air design generally consists of a metallic (aluminum or steel) housing, although sometimes the housing is made of plastic. This holds the GPU and their PCIE-riser card which is tightly placed close to the motherboard and PSU. In older systems, you may require two PSUs as the GPU power consumption may be high (sometimes up to 300 watts for each GPU), but as I said earlier, even with six AMD Radeon RX 470 4GB, you would not require more than 1000 watts. But the other reason why you may need a second PSU is in order to mount the GPUs in a different location, not just next to the motherboard. This will require longer USB cables for the PCIE-riser card (read more on this in the section on PCIE-riser card).

Design #1: Chassis made of aluminum cube channels, or U profile.

Space-saving system: You can create a grid of rigs in any horizontal or vertical configuration if you want to. U or C channels can be easily found online or in any local metal or furniture shop. They are easy to work with, and flexible to shape and assemble, and also offer great rigidity. The key here is the distance between each GPU. The ideal distance is 10 cm or about 4 inches. At less than 10 cm, the heat from one GPU will affect the other; at more than 10 cm, the space will be wasted. In most of the open-air systems, GPUs are mounted on the chassis by two screws on the rear video-card bracket and the PCIE connectors are left unattached to the ground or base unlike a typical computer case which has two attachment points, viz. the PCIE slot and rear video-card bracket[4].

---

[4] As elsewhere in this book, click on the hyperlink to go to the reference. The references are also listed in the reference section. Please note that I take no credit or responsibility for the validity of the material in the references, although they do appear reliable to me.

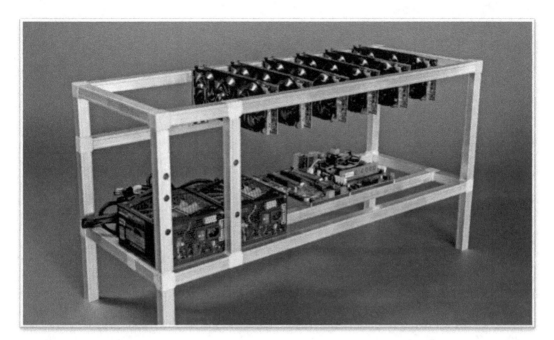

Figure 1 - Picture of a mining rig with 6 GPUs. As the GPUs are power hungry, they require two power supplies. Reference <u>here</u>!

Figure 2 - This is a picture of a small mining farm, with 6 mining rigs, each has 4–5 GPUs. Note that the system is very clean. Note also that the place must have good ventilation and with only ceramic tiles on the floor and walls. The room will however be very noisy. Reference is <u>here</u>.

There are companies that have mastered some very interesting and nice designs and the sell them online. One of them is named "Flow 6.1" and is from MintCell. It has a vertically mounted GPU design in a very compact and neat form. For more information, go to eBay.com, Amazon.com or Newegg.com and visit the product page.

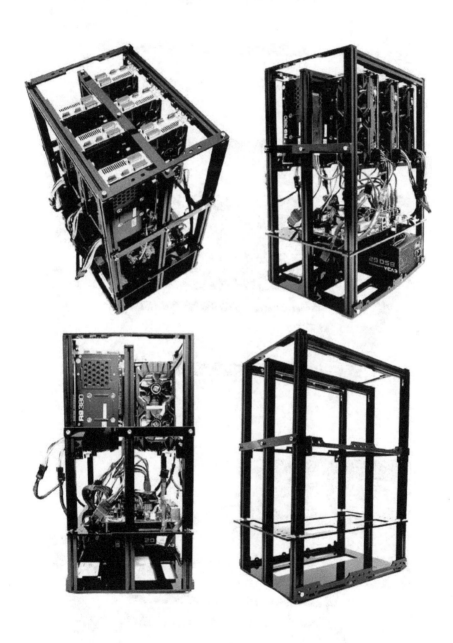

There are some companies that build the GPU mining system professionally and sell them online, e.g., in Europe, visit website of ethereumminer.eu for an affordable chassis that can hold up to six GPUs.

Figure 3 - A GPU-miner chassis, open-air design from the Netherlands, see ethereumminer.eu. Reference is here!

Here is another neat and well-designed GPU mining chassis from a company called "Gadget Saloon". I found it on eBay.com where it is indicated that it can hold 6 graphics (video) cards, 1 motherboard (ATX/MATX), 6 cooling fans and a temperature monitoring LCD panel. I have not seen any reviews or comments on this chassis design but its look very practical. Please refer to this link to get more information!

Figure 4 - This is a mining-rig system in a plastic tray. It is practical but looks messy and doesn't offer good rigidity. The GPUs are too close together which affects their cooling. However, it is very cheap and easy to build and it does the job which is to hold the GPUs in place! Reference is <u>here</u>!

On most of the open-air style chassis, the GPUs are fixed using the rear bracket of the GPU. There are two screws to fix this to a normal computer case. The bottom of the card hangs loosely in air where PCIE express-riser card sits. The picture below shows a similar design. This is a well-made GPU mining rig with six units of Sapphire Nitro Radeon RX 480 8GB on an Asrock motherboard. The chassis is simple: it is made out of aluminium square rectangular tubes specifically for a GPU mining rig.

In another design, see <u>online post in imgur</u>, I found a very well-built and organized GPU miner which I believe is built on a shoe rack or similar item.

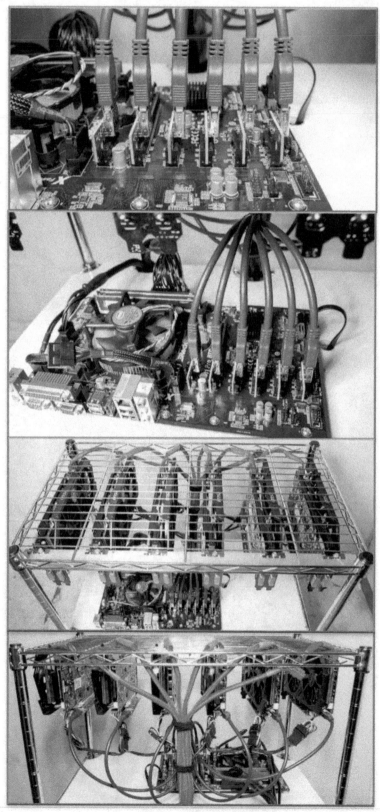

5.1.2. Closed-air design

A typical computer case is considered as a closed-air design, where the components and the GPUs are enclosed within a case, box or container. In a closed-air design, the only openings are designated air channels for the entrance and exit of ventilating air. The air channels usually have fan-mounting holes to which cooling fans can be fitted.

Figure 5 - Corsair 100R mid-tower case from 3 different views. This is a perfect case for a mining rig with maximum of 2 GPUs, link is here!

In the past, I managed to fit four maximum GPUs in a mining rig with a giant full-tower case. Two of the GPUs were installed on PCIE X16 slots and two were connected by USB3 PCIE-riser cards. The reason for doing this was only in order to control the noise with a closed enclosure and also to eliminate the dust.

The advantages of a closed-air design over an open-air design are:

1. Better control of dust—the dust filters can be placed on the air intake and trap the dust properly.
2. Better noise suppression and much more suitable for non-industrial environments, such as a house or school, or when there is only one or a few GPU miners working.
3. Better control on air delivery and air exhaustion. Yes, better control, but less air delivery due to restrictions.

The disadvantages of a closed-air mining rig:

1. More complex design and usually more expensive than an open-air system.
2. Less air delivery as the GPUs are entrapped in a tighter space, have less room to "breathe" freely, and the walls of the case make it more restricted.
3. If the external fans fail, the GPU miner runs very poorly as the GPUs' core temperature rises very rapidly and would shut down or the core clock would throttle down (this reduces the performance).
4. Not suitable for industrial use or a large mining farm. In a mining farm, the noise of the GPU miner doesn't matter, and as mining farm produces lots heat, there is well-designed ventilation system in charge of delivery of fresh air and exhausting of warm air. A ventilation system also can also be used to manage the air filtration using some industrialized air filters. A closed-air chassis uses its own simple air filtration system just before the intake fans.

Let's get back to the closed-air design. How do we make one? What you need in order to build a closed-air mining rig are the following:

1. A big box made out of wood or metal. A metallic box would however be hard to reshape, cut or make holes in.
2. The components of a mining rig.
3. Fans and air filters.

Usually, I made my closed-air mining rigs out of used cabinets, shelves, boxes, commodes, etc. The best option on these is a small two-section cabinet made of wood with a door. Below picture shows a TV table with wheel, which is ideal to place motherboard and GPUs on different shelves.

Figure 6 - This is an old wooden cabinet with door. It has enough space for a miner with three to four GPUs. By adding another shelf, it could take a total of 6 GPUs in two stories.

wooden shelf is my favorite to use because:

1. It is easy to get for free or very cheaply. In any neighborhood, you may find old and unwanted furniture for free, or buy them cheaply. There is no need to worry about the appearance—the look isn't important at all, so, a scratched, old and tarnished one would be just fine.
2. You can modify the body easily, drill holes in it, take parts off or add an extra shelf.
3. Wood is an electrical, sound and heat insulator, so the GPUs and PCIE risers can be directly screwed to it. Wood also damps some of the noise.

At the professional level, there are companies that design and build server racks or professional computers for graphical or mining purposes.

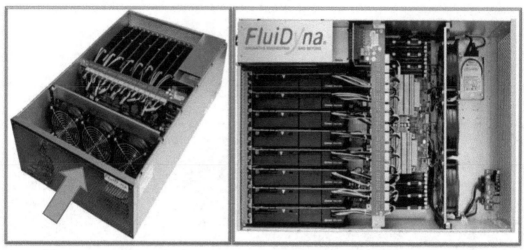

Figure 7 - This is a picture of a server computer with 8 Nvidia Quadro GPUs. It is not suitable as a GPU-miner as the GPUs would be too close to each other and would not allow enough fresh air to circulate. In addition, blower-style GPUs are not suitable for mining purposes as they have inferior cooling abilities. Link is here! And here!

As I said earlier, the main goal of a closed-air design is to control **dust** and **noise** and without these two main advantages, this design has poorer characteristics in performance than open-air design.

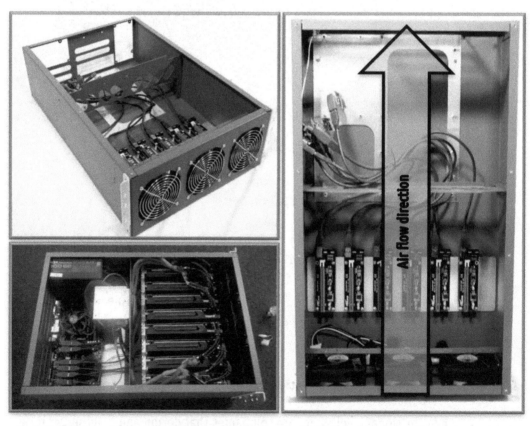

Figure 8 - This is a neat design called "GrayMatter GPU Server Case V2.1" from miningrigs.net. It can accommodate 6 GPUs, but does not have the air-intake filtration, link is here!

The advantage of a custom-made mining rig is that you can customize the cooling fans too, or you can buy an empty well-made mining chassis and add your own components. Most mining-rig chassis don't come with an active air filter which is very important for me. Also, server-grade cooling fans rotate at high speed and are very noisy.

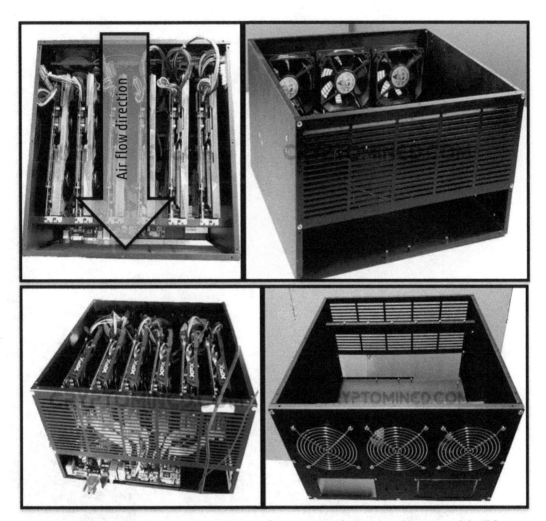

Figure 9 - This is a 6-GPU MINING-RIG CASE WITH 3 FANS from cryptomined.com. It has a big open mesh (grill) for exhaust. Link is here!

To complete a closed-air mining rig, you may need to cut, drill or modify your custom-made mining-rig case, which could require some expertise and could be time consuming.

Here is a custom-made mining rig with 8 GPUs and two motherboards which I built inside of an IKEA shelf. The backplate of the shelf is not original; I made that out of thin plywood as the original backplate was too thick to cut and drill in order to make holes for all of the fans. Most of the fans are F12 Arctic PWM, but one is a 150-mm low-noise 220-V fan, which is at the bottom.

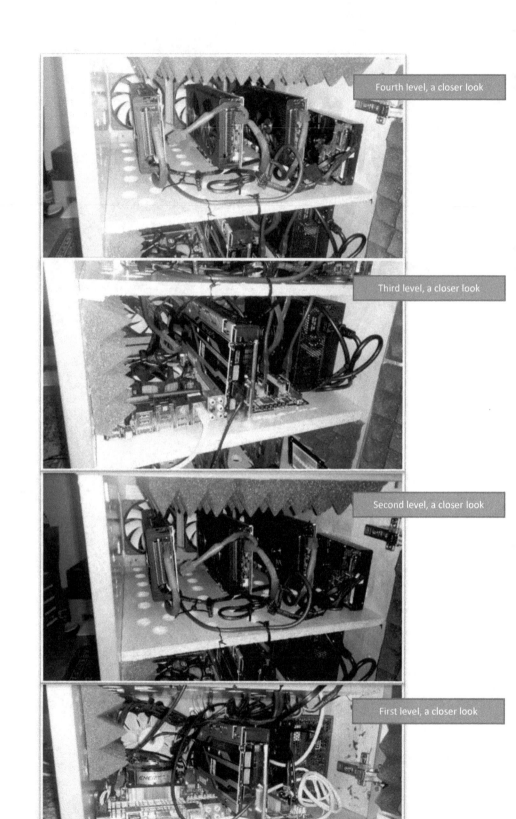

Fourth level, a closer look

Third level, a closer look

Second level, a closer look

First level, a closer look

5.2. Building a GPU mining rig based on certain budget

All mining rigs consist of a desktop computer that is equipped with a rather powerful graphics card. As explained earlier, at the moment Nvidia 900s GPUs are not suitable for mining purposes as:

1. Nvidia graphic card aren't optimized for GPU mining software. Mining software doesn't utilize the potential of the GPU as much as some 3D software does, for instance, in the last few years, in playing games Nvidia GPUs perform better than their AMD rivals. Furthermore, the AMD and Nvidia graphic cards have different microarchitecture designs. They are also unlike on how to process the instructions while they have different number Arithmetic/Logic Units(ALUs), subsequently. So, mining algorithms of Ethereum (and similar GPU mining-software) platform, usually AMD GPUs outperform similar class Nvidia GPUs[5] [1].

2. For a similar performance, you can buy an AMD GPU at half the price. For instance, a Nvidia GeForce 1070 8GB has a similar performance to an AMD Radeon RX 470 4GB in GPU mining in Linux OS[6]. However, in May 2017 after increase on price of many GPU-mining-friendly cryptocoins such Ether, Siacoin, Pascal, Zencoin, Zcash, etc. many has attracted to this business. This matter increased the demand of AMD GPUs exponentially and in most of places AMD GPUs are not to be found, all are out of stock even Radeon RX 460 and RX 560. So, people start trying to work on what available on hand from Nvidia, this is how mining with Nvidia GTX 1060 has reborn. I'll come back to Nvidia GTX 1060 later in the chapter and in Chapter 6 as well.

3. By design, the Nvidia architecture is different from that of AMD. AMD designs GPUs with many simple ALUs/shaders that run at a relatively low-frequency clock, whereas Nvidia's microarchitecture consists of fewer more-complex ALUs and tries to compensate with a higher-shader clock.

Here in this section, I have divided the mining rigs according to the total cost of the system, starting at $100, which is almost the lowest amount you can pay for an old desktop computer. Any desktop computer with a discrete graphics card can be used for GPU mining. Later on, this chapter, I have considered other options using more

---

[5] Read more about "Why are AMD GPUs faster than Nvidia GPUs?" in the online article here!
[6] To avoid confusion, performance of a GPU here is related to its hashing power, not how well it runs 3D software or a game, so AMD GPU has superior performance relative to its rival Nvidia (i.e. the AMD GPU makes more hashes per second).

GPUs. Most desktop computers are not able to run more than one GPU because of restrictions on space or limitation of power supply.

5.2.1. Cheapest option: total cost below $100

So, we have $100 budget for a mining rig. What we need are:

1. A motherboard with one available PCIE slot, including CPU and 4 GB RAM.
2. A hard drive storage with 120 GB or more.
3. A PSU with 300 W or more.
4. A case, fan, etc.
5. A GPU with mining capabilities (this is the most important part).

For items 1, 2, 3 and 4, I recommend that you buy a used working PC and paying attention to the following points:

1. The power supply should be at least 300 W (the bigger, the better), preferably with PCIE 6 and 8 pin connectors (this is not a must as Molex to PCIE adaptors can be used).
2. If the PC comes with a hard drive, it is better that it already has Windows 7 OS on it which is the easiest OS that you can use for mining, and can be set up for the mining rig in an hour.
3. Case and case fans aren't so important; a bigger case is better and has more room for ventilation. You will of course have the benefit of a lower temperature if you have more case fans.

A working PC with a Pentium Core 2 Duo or Quad with DDR2 and DDR3, sometimes even newer, can easily be purchased for $20–$50 from your local used PC shops or online sellers, such as eBay. Deducting this from our initial investment of $100, we have $50–$80 left in our budget for a GPU.

You need to pay attention to the fact that Ethereum mining requires a GPU with at least 3 GB of memory (I explained this in Chapter 2, GPU section). Although you may be able to run your mining software with some tricks and modification with a GPU with 2 GB RAM this is not recommended. With a budget of $50–80, we have the following options:

AMD R9 270X 2 GB, AMD 7950 3 GB, AMD 7970 3 GB, AMD R9 280 3 GB, AMD R9 280X 3 GB, R9 280 4 GB, etc.

You need to find a clean, used card in good working order. Buying a used GPU is always a tricky business but as our budget is tight, we cannot buy a new card. Always try to test the card before you buy, if you cannot return it later. I recommend that you buy an R9 series of AMD card rather than the 7000s series, as they are newer, have a higher clock and most probably have less mileage on them.

As of May 2017, R9 270X is being sold for around $50–60 in my local market and it gives around 12 MH/s, the problem in June 2017 was: all of AMD GPUs are on high demand and they are either overpriced or not available to buy. R9 270X has a TDP of 180 W and usually requires two of the 6-pin[7] PCIE power connectors (sometimes one 8-pin and one 6-pin). Your system will consume around 300 watts of energy under load. How much can you make with it? With an Ether (ETH) price of $8.3 and the earnings will be around $13 after a month but your electricity bill will be $24, so you are going to lose some money with it. But as the price of Ether has increased to around $50 in April 2017, and network hash rate has increased to 16,517 GH/s, the calculated earnings will be $33. After deducting $24 for the cost of the power, you would be left with a $9 profit by the end of the month.

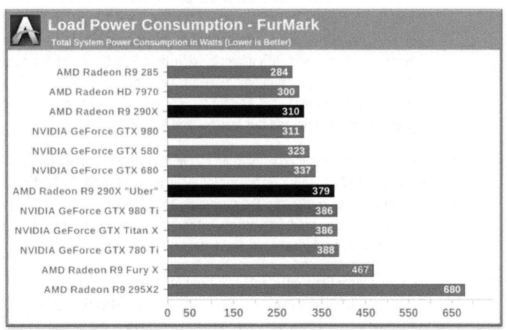

Figure 10 - Load power consumption of high-end GPUs in 2015. This was taken from the **Anandtech.com** website, when the GPU was running under FurMark torture software, link is here!

---

[7] As said Chapter 3, with a high-performance GPU, you can get the extra power through PCIE connectors directly from power supply. These PCIE connectors usually come in 6-pin and 8-pin variation sockets. Official power delivery of 6-pin and 8-pin power cables are 75 watts and 150 watts, respectively.

How about the R9 280X? This makes 16–18 MH/s with a core clock of around 1000 MHz. The total power drawn from the system is around 350 watts, so your earnings with 18 MH/s would be around $22 and your power cost would be around $30 at the end of the first month. You would therefore make a loss of around $8! Disappointed? As I explained in Chapter 4, the price of Ether has been around the unfair value of $8 since November 2016 and the relative network difficulty has been high. Let's calculate the profit again with the new price of Ether (ETH) of over $50. With 18 MH/s and a power rating of 350 W at price of $0.12 per watthours, a network hash rate of 16,517 GH/s and the price of ETH of $52.47, you would earn ~$50 by the end of the month. The cost of power would be $30, so the profit would be about $20.

So, many of the GPU miners who are using the 200s or 300s series AMD of GPUs such as Radeon R9 280X, R9 390 and R9 390X, haven't been earning very much. The mining rig won't make a profit until:

1. You use more efficient GPUs.
2. The price of ETH or ETC increases. The price of ETH would need to go above $12 as it did in March 2017, where it reached above $50.
3. You utilize the heat that comes out of the system, for instance, for heating your room. As I explained in Chapters 3 and 4, most of the time in cold climates, you pay for heating your home, whether your house heating system works with gas or electricity. If you can reuse the heat that comes out of your mining rig to warm your room and thereby let you turn off or turn down your normal form of heating, then you will save yourself some money and this may put you in profit.

If you have access to cheap electricity, then this mining rig would work for you—it would make $10–$20 a month from your initial investment of $100, which isn't that bad. You could of course run the system on an experimental basis, just to earn some cryptocurrency and determine whether mining works for you. Such an experimental system would make sense as it doesn't cost much.

However, things were little different at the end of June 2017, where 1 ETH was $328.27. The calculated profit of system is ~$33, where network hash rate of 53,265 GH/s, and system consumes 350W on $ 0.12 per kWh.

So, things are getting really promising with the new increased-price of cryptocoins, not only Ether is profitable, but many others join the Ethereum to offer some earnings. Check www.whattomine.com where offers a good comparison on the profit on mining different cryptocurrencies.

Figure 11- Picture of HP XW4600T Workstation, with two PCI Express (PCIe) x16 graphics slots. Unusually comes with a powerful 475 W PSU.

After the increase demand on AMD Radeon RX 470, 480, 570 and 580, they have been out of stock in June 2017, people start to pay more attention to their Nvidia counterparts again, GTX 1050ti and 1060. Why these two only? Well first comes with the price range, where 1050ti is being sold for $139-$169 in July 2017. GTX 1060 3 GB can be found as low as $199 up to ~$300 for 6 GB models, and over $300 for new recent 1060 6GB 9GB/s fast memory versions[8]. Where GTX 1070 enters to the ~$400 territory and the mining power is not so significant.

On normal GPU mining conditions without tweaks and overclocks, GTX 1050ti hashes Ether about 10-12MH/s, and GTX 1060 3 GB make about 16-18 MH/s, and 6 GB versions with 9Gbps mines about 17-19 MH/s. A AMD Radeon RX 560 4GB which is priced $100-$140 mines about 12-14 MH/s easily without hassle. A tweaked RX 570 can mine about 22-26 MH/s. The good news on Nvidia side is, GTX 1050ti and 1060 are much more efficient than AMD GPUs. Few Nvidia 1050ti cards come

---

[8] The regular Nvidia GTX 1060 6 GB cards usually come with GDDR5 memory with data transfer rate of 8Gbps, and on 2017, GDDR5X is being added to the lineup with 9Gbps.

without any PCIE power connectors, made them perfect for your experimental and cheap GPU mining rig.

SFX power supply 250W, not so suitable for GPU mining Job

2 available PCIE slot, X16 and one X1

Figure 12 - Picture of Fujitsu ESPRIMO E3521 with Core2Duo CPU, the power supply is not strong enough for a high TDP GPU to run, the whole system can be purchased less than ~$50

Here, in the pictures below, is another good example of an old desktop computer, which can be purchased for $50–$100 depending on the CPU configuration (whether 2nd or 3rd generation Intel). It has three PCI Express slots but only one full-sized GPU can be fitted inside of the case, as it has one X16 and two X1 size PCIE slots. The main problem with any ordinary desktop computer is that: for GPU mining the power supply that comes with desktop computer is usually insufficient, being rated below 300 W. Furthermore, the power supply does not have PCIE power connectors for a discrete GPU. Usually, the power supply unit (PSU) must be changed to be able to run a GPU card and therefore operate in mining.

Figure 13 - This is IBM Lenovo ThinkCentre EDGE71 SOCKET 1155 MOTHERBOARD. On the second-hand market like eBay, it can be purchased for $50–$100.

5.2.2. Next option with one or two GPUs, total cost $200–$700

The component requirements are similar to the first option below $100, but there are a few points to note. If you aim to spend $200, you have 2 options: 1. Either to go for a new graphics card, an AMD Radeon RX 460 4GB or an Radeon RX 470 4GB, or 2. Two of the AMD R9 300s or 200s series. The cost of power would be less for the first option. As we saw in the $100 GPU mining build, the second option with AMD R9 300s or older series cards is not profitable when the Ether (ETH) price is low.

Here is an example of a mining rig costing around $200 with the following components and requirements:

1. A motherboard with 2 available PCIE X16 slots with a CPU and 4 GB RAM (8 GB would be better) plus a Case and Hard Disk Drive (HDD) also with Operating System (OS) = $50
2. Two R9 270X, or R9 280X or similar cards, or a combination of these, as the GPU model does not need to be the same necessarily, for instance, a AMD R9 270X and R9 380 can work together in a GPU mining system, although I do not recommend it. Always it's better to get two or more similar GPUs in a GPU mining rig.
3. A power supply (PSU) with power rating of at least 600 W [2]. This is usually hard to find in a used PC that costs around $50-$100. So, you will most probably end up with buying a new or used budget 600+ W PSU. Your PSU must have PCIE power connectors but, if it doesn't come with PCIE power connectors, you should use a Molex to PCIE adaptor. Nevertheless, you cannot supply power to two power-hungry GPUs from Molex power connectors. So, to make the story short only buy a PSU that comes with PCIE cables natively.
4. Your case should be big enough to accommodate two GPUs. Many cases are not suitable for big GPUs because the ventilation is poor and the heat generated would hurt your mining performance.

This option is only viable when you have access to cheap electricity, or you can make use of the heat generated.

A wiser option would be to use the following:

1. The same old used PC as with the $100 option.

2. An AMD RX 460 4 GB, which should cost $120–140 or a AMD RX 470 4 GB, which should cost $160–200

The AMD RX 460 has a TDP of 75 W, and the total power consumption of the system under load would be about 180 watts [3]. The AMD Radeon RX 460 can hash about 12 MH/s, which is similar to the old R9 270X. But let's calculate the earnings now with a power consumption of 180 watts and a hash rate of 12 MH/s. The power would cost around $15.5, which is just about the same amount of money that you would make with an Ether price of $8.5. Now we are talking! If the price were $12, we would make about $5–$10 per month! In March 2017, with a network hash rate of 16,627 GH/s and an Ether price of $52.6, a rig hashing power of 12 MH/s, and a power usage of 180 watts, we would make $33 in a month, and the profit would be $17.25 in that month. As I said earlier, the received Ether will reduce over the next months as the network hash rate increases, because the same amount of Ether will need to be shared with more miners.

Let's get back to our build but with a **GPU mining champion card: AMD Radeon RX 470 4GB**. As I explained in Chapters 2 and 3, at the begging of 2017, the AMD Radeon RX 470 4GB has the best price and the best performance per watt. Even if I wanted to build a mining rig with 100 GPUs, I would still go for the AMD Radeon RX 470 4GB. The GPU power consumption is around 120 watts per GPU units, and 100 watts overall for the rest of the components of the system including motherboard, CPU and RAM, etc. So, total consumption is about 220 watts, although these 220 watts depend on the motherboard and CPU generation and efficiency and can be varied by 20%. The AMD Radeon RX 470 can continuously mine with an average hash rate of 20 MH/s with peaks of 22 MH/s and lows of 16 MH/s. Unlike the previous generation, the core-clock management is much more dynamic and, during the Ethereum mining operation I have experienced inconsistencies in the performance of the AMD RX series graphics cards. During November 2016 until February 2017 when the 1 ETH was exchanged with $8.5, and a power consumption of 220 watts at price of $0.12/kWh, the rig with a Radeon RX 470 can make a profit of around $10 in a month (power cost has been deducted). Again, as of April 2017, when the network hash rate was 16,627 GH/s and the ETH price was $52.6, the monthly profit was $35.66.

Why isn't it more? The reasons are:

1. The system isn't efficient enough with a power consumption of 100 watts for the non-GPU components.

2. We have only one GPU in the system; adding extra GPUs would leverage the cost of power consumption of the non-GPU components.
3. The price of the ETH was surprisingly low at around $10, while the block difficulty was relatively high. So, the earnings would not be good. When the price rose to more than $50 in March 2017, the profit was relatively high.
4. The heat of the mining rig is assumed to be wasted. If some of the heat could be reused, then this would make the system more economic.

Let's add one more RX 470 4GB. The cost of the mining system with two new AMD RX 470 4GB would be about $450. What are the complications?

1. As a Radeon RX 470 takes a power consumption of 120 watts, you would need a PSU that could provide a minimum 350–400 W. The AMD Radeon RX 470 4GB would require one 6-pin or one 8-pin PCIE power connector depending on the brand. If the PSU doesn't come with pair of PCIE power connectors, the power delivery can be provided with a Molex to PCIE adaptor as any PSU does come with many Molex power connector natively. But, I do not recommend using Molex connectors for power delivery to the GPU. So, try to get a decent PSU with a pair of native PCIE power connectors which does not cost more than $50, as you are spending about $400 on the GPUs.
2. The motherboard should have PCIE X16 slots available. If there aren't two such slots but there is one X8, X4 or X1, you will require a PCIE-riser card which would cost an additional $10.
3. Your case, or chassis should have sufficient space to accommodate two AMD Radeon RX 470 4GB. Your case should have enough "breathing space" and should be able to provide an adequate air flow for the GPUs.

How much can you make with this system?

The power consumption of system would be about 100 watts for the system components and 120 watts for each GPU, of which there are two. This makes a total power requirement of 320–350 W. The profit from a 32–40 MH/s GPU mining rig with the ETH price of $8.5, and a power cost of $0.12/kWh would be about $23 in a month[9]. Not bad! We are getting somewhere. Now let's calculate the profit

---

[9] You may use any of the Ethereum or Ethereum classic profit calculators online. I recommended some of them in Chapter 4. Don't be fooled by one-year profit predications or promises of a return on your investment in X days! These are not accurate as the difficulty growth is fixed. Every day, more and more miners come online and the share of the cryptocurrency earning would get smaller if the price had not increased during the previous 6 month! Go for predictions with dynamic difficulty, see Chapter 4.

again with a network hash rate of 16,604 GH/s and using an ETH price of $52.38. In this case, the earnings would be $109 with profit of $78.79. The cost of the system "Ex02-1150-Rev01"[10] is around €750. I have chosen a 450 W PSU that can provide power to up to 3 units of AMD Radeon RX 470 4GB. You can find the details and Excel files in the Appendix.

If you are not planning to enter the GPU mining world seriously, it would be better to start with a good used PC and a new GPU(s). If you decide later to quit mining, you should be able to sell these items easily.

Figure 14 - This is a picture of a desktop computer with two RX 480 reference design in a Full ATX Thermaltake case. The picture is taken from a reddit post, link is here!

The above picture shows that in an ordinary computer case, the GPUs would be placed so close to each other that the cooling would not be ideal. In addition, two X16 PCIE slots should be available on the motherboard.

---

[10] In this book, I have prepared samples of a GPU mining rig with a different number of GPUs and configurations. Ex02-1150-Rev01, Ex stands for example, 02 indicates the number of GPUs, 1150 is the intel socket number, and Rev01 is the revision 01. The complete detail of these systems can be found at the end of the book in the Appendix.

5.2.3. Mining rig with three GPUs, total cost ~$1000

The mining rig with 3 GPUs, for instance, the "Ex03-1150-Rev01"[11] system, has 3 AMD RX 470 4GB, two of which must be mounted on the PCIE-riser cards. If you have a full-tower case, you may still be able to fix your GPUs inside it. However, we will start with a custom-made mining-rig chassis. A regular computer case has lots of restrictions and most of the time you can't place extra GPUs inside it unless you unmount some of the HDD bays and trays. Also, the cooling won't be perfect. The pictures below are taken from an article "AMD RADEON RX 480 3-Ways CROSSFIRE SHOWTIME", which was published in Vmodtech.com [4]. They illustrate how you might place four RX 480 of the reference design together. At the moment, only X99 chipset full-size motherboards offer four X16 PCIE lanes.

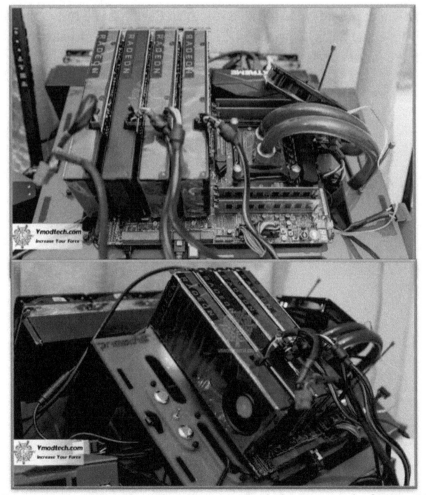

Figure 15 - This is a 3-way crossfire configuration on a test bench. The picture was taken from an article on the Vmodtech.com blog. Here you can see when the PCIE riser is not being used in a mining rig The GPUs must be placed very tightly together.

---

[11] As it explained before, this system has three GPUs and is based on an intel 1150 CPU socket.

The price of the Ex03-1150-Rev01 is around €1000 in May 2017. A PSU that can provide about 500 watts is adequate for 3 AMD Radeon RX 470 4GB GPUs. How much would be your earnings? As of January 2017, statistics with the ETH price of $9.83, a difficulty of ~92 trillions, and a power consumption is 450 watts at a cost of $0.12/kWh, the earnings would be ~$50 in the first month and $150–$250 in 6 month[12].

The cost of the GPUs in the ideal scenario, which has five or six GPUs per miner, would be **68–70%** of the cost of the entire system. A higher ratio of GPU cost to total system cost indicates a better utilization of the money in a GPU mining rig. Why? The purpose of any components of a GPU mining rig is to let the GPUs run, so that when you save the cost of the other components, the total cost for a GPU-miner is less cheap and the GPU-miner becomes more profitable. With a 3-GPU system consisting of Ex03-1150-Rev01, the ratio of the GPU cost to the total cost is at 64%, so your system is 64/70, i.e. 91%, efficient when compared with an ideal 6-GPU miner.

---

[12] As I've already said, the earnings would depend very much on the ETH or ETC price, the block difficulty, the number of active miners and the hash rate. I use an online calculator with dynamic growth of block difficulty. You can of course make your own predictions using the links that I've provided. The results will change from day to day. The numbers and predictions here are only examples to show how the system works.

5.2.4. Mining rig with more than 5 GPUs: total cost over $2000

When we analyze a GPU mining rig from the cost efficiency and utilization of the GPU perspective, a mining rig with five or six GPUs has the maximum utilization of cost of GPUs per cost of a mining rig (~70% of the total cost, as explained in previous section). <u>In a regular desktop motherboard</u>, with 1150 or 1151 Intel socket motherboards, like those that we use in a GPU mining rig, we have the maximum number of six PCIE slots. Usually one or two of them are X16-size sockets[13], and rest are smaller and mostly X1-size sockets. There are some <u>server motherboards</u> that offer more than 6 PCIE slots. For instance, the Fujitsu Primergy TX300 S5, Mainboard type D 2619 [5] has 7 PCIE slots and can be purchased for around €60 [6], but the total cost of the system including the Intel socket 1366 CPU(s), RAM, etc. would go up to ~€400.

Figure 16 - A picture of the Fujitsu Primergy TX300 S, Socket 1366, Mainboard type D 2619 motherboard with 7 PCIE X8 slots.

---

[13] PCIE express socket on a motherboard comes with a standard size of X1, X4, X8 and X16. A modern GPU requires X16 PCIE express socket size.

When you have made your decision on the total number of GPUs you want to have in your rig, the total cost of system will also depend on how much you spend on the mining-rig chassis. As I have explained in the section on chassis design, it may cost less than $20 for a metal or wooden custom-made one or up to $300 for a very well-made aluminum or steel one. Always remember that the less you spend on the non-GPU components and parts, the better. You will need to minimize the cost while achieving the design goals, which are:

1. Running the mining rig non-stop 24/7.
2. Providing a decent cooling and ventilation in order to manage GPU-core temperature below 80° C.
3. Being efficient—using a PSU of Gold 80 or better and a low-powered CPU and motherboard.

In the next sections, I'm going to introduce possible GPU mining builds with number of GPU to maximum of nine!!

5.2.5. A mining rig with six GPUs

In a GPU mining rig, the utilization of your CPU is usually below 20%, while the utilization of your PSU is 90% or higher, so when you do your research for the components, look for efficiency of the power supply at 85–95% utilization. As explained in Chapter 2, every PSU manufacturer provides an efficiency chart or table based on the utilization of the power supply. The maximum TDP of your CPU is irrelevant but you will need to look at the idle power consumption of the total system. There are many articles in which you can read about the total power consumption of the system in idle mode. Note that your CPU remains idle while your GPUs are working at 100%.

Let's do the calculation for the "Ex06-1150-Rev01" system with six of AMD RX 470 4GB GPUs. The total cost of the system is ~€1850 in March 2017. With the value of the ETH at $9.83, a difficulty of ~94.8 trillion, a power consumption of 850 watts at a cost of $0.1/kWh, and a hash rate of 120–150 MH/s, the profit would be ~$90 in first month and $275–$400[14] in 6 months (these values depend on block difficulty). On April 4, 2017, mining metrics were calculated based on a network hash rate of 17,159 GH/s and using a price for the ETH of $44.8, a difficulty of 241.6933 trillion, and a power consumption of 850 watts at a cost of $0.12/kWh, the profit from a 150 MH/s GPU mining rig would have been $264.93 in a month.

---

[14] As I said earlier as of today, dollar and euro are so close together (10% difference), so you may use only euros or dollar for your own calculations.

Based on the "Carl Diab" calculator, the predicated income over a 6-month period with difficulty increasing by 80 million per month would be around $650.

But I mentioned many times, the price of Ether jumped by 400% to ~$50 from February to end of March 2017, and then again increased by another 400% from March to June 2017 to around ~ $243 on 5th of June 2017. Remember that, the calculations here on profit and earning, may not be updated at the time you are reading this book, so always do the calculations with the updated information on price of Ether(ETH), network total hash power and block difficulty. Always try to use multiple online calculators to ensure about your results. The calculations which is mentioned here are just to guide you the method of figuring out the income and cost, and are as examples, at the end you need to do the homework yourself.

In the past, during 2015-2016, a six GPUs mining rig configuration was the sweet spot of all GPU mining rigs, why? Well the best mining GPUs were AMD R9 series, Radeon R9 280X, 290, 290X, 380X, 390 and 390X. These GPUs have TDP of around 200W, so the total system draw with six of them was ~1500-1600W which is the maximum you can find on a single PSU. Besides, prior to 2016, the design of PCIE riser cards were different, using direct transfer technology rather than USB3, and, most of them were not powered. So, PCIE raiser card used to draw pretty high power from a PCIE slot, so ordinary motherboards that did not have an extra power input usually in form of MOLEX, were not able to run 5 or 6 six GPUs with this configuration and were not stable in mining operation. So, motherboards like ASRock H81 Pro BTC has created that has two extra Molex type power input, to ensure power supply on the PCIE slots. However, the new generation of USB3 PCIE riser card does have a Molex power input and it is powered, so it does not draw so much power from motherboard PCIE slot. This matter allows any regular motherboard to be suitable for a GPU mining rig build. Here, I'm going to skip on PCIE riser cards, as you will read more about it at the end of Chapter 5 and 6.

For a complete build guide please proceed to Chapter 6.

5.2.6. A mining rig with seven GPUs

As I said using more than six GPUs in a GPU mining rig uncommon, why?

1. There are few desktop motherboards available that has more than six PCIE slots.

2. Having six or seven PCIE slots does not make a motherboard: mining friendly, most of motherboards are not designed to have all PCIE slots occupied, they only offer different slot placements in different computer build configurations. Consequently, if you hook them with six or more GPUs, they don't work or may not be stable.
3. The power draw of a GPU mining rig with more than six GPUs is close to maximum threshold of a single PSU, ~1300W-1600W, and using a second PSU is not so welcomed in modern designs of GPU mining rigs.

Any regular desktop motherboard that has 6 available PCIE lots and a M.2 expansion slot, can accommodate seven GPUs. MSI B250 KRAIT Gaming, Asus Prime H270-Plus, MSI Z270 SLI Plus, GIGABYTE GA-Z270-Gaming K3 or MSI Z270-A Pro are some examples of them. There are six available PCIE slots available on these motherboards, and the seventh GPU will be connected through M.2 slot. A PCIE 4X Female to NGFF M.2 M Key Male Adapter is being used to connect graphics card to the motherboard. Read more about it in this Chapter, in Accessories section.

However, Asus Prime Z270-A Gaming Mainboard with socket 1151, has seven available PCIE slots, so on theory there is possibility of connecting seven GPUs to this motherboard without using any M.2 expansion slots.

Based on this motherboard, I have setup a seven GPUs mining rig of "Ex07-1151-Rev01" where you can find the details in the Appendix Chapter.

In a "Bits Be Trippin" YouTube channel, I have seen a build that this motherboard is being used to make a GPU mining rig with nine GPUs, connecting two of GPUs through M.2 expansion slots. In that particular build, rig draws ~1560W and makes ~264 MH/s with nine AMD Radeon RX 580 cards.

The other option on building a more-than-six GPU mining rig is using non-desktop configurations. In this case, we need to move to using a server-board machine. Server motherboards are those that have 7 available PCIE slots and usually come with dual CPU-socket configurations. This makes them more expensive. I recommend you use a socket 1366 motherboard because a socket 771 is too old with a DDR2 RAM and doesn't come with the required PCIE lanes and performance, and sockets 2011 or 2011–3 cost more than $400 now, although these would also provide a stable and modern system.

If you have decided to try a 1366-socket system, always try to get a complete server computer rather than parts. The reason for this is that a server motherboard, especially the OEM version, has more complexity than a desktop machine, and may not be compatible with custom CPUs or RAM. In addition, the system requires a pair of CPU coolers as it has two CPUs (one cooler for each CPU) and some motherboards do not work with a single CPU configuration. The best option is always to get a used clean working server machine.

A Fujitsu PRIMERGY RX300 S6 [7] has a D2619-N15 GS1 motherboard, which costs ~€100 [8], although a complete system can be found from around €200 on eBay (link is here)[15]. The recommended RAM for a 7-GPU mining rig is 16 GB, and a server motherboard requires ECC RAM modules.

The good thing about server systems, which usually use Xeon CPUs, is that they have a lower TDP than desktop CPUs, and they also operate at a lower temperature. The RX300 S6 with two Xeon 6-core-X5650 CPUs (each CPU uses 95 watts on 100% load) runs on idle with 3 HDDs that use 136 watts [9]. The best socket, 1366, for a mining rig is Xeon L5609 with a 40-W TDP, or similar Xeons. You can choose from the Intel website [10], link is here The average power consumption would be 900–950 watts. So, with the "Ex07-1150-Rev01" system with 7 AMD RX 470 4GB GPUs, the total cost of the system would be ~€2150. With a

---

[15] eBay links are not valid for a long time. Usually, they are available for a month. So, you will need to search with the right search phrase, for example, "Fujitsu PRIMERGY RX300 S6".

value of ETH of $10.05, a difficulty of ~93.2 trillion, a power consumption of 950 watts at a cost of $0.1/kWh, and a hash rate of around 140–165 MH/s, the earnings would be ~$105 in the first month and $350–$530 in 6 months (depending on block difficulty).

As the price of Ether increased to $44.18 on April 4, 2017, the earnings from the "Ex07-1150-Rev01" would be ~$366 in the first month, with a network hash rate of 17,184 GH/s and a difficulty of 243.4162 trillion. As the cost of electricity (950 watts supply) would be $82.08 at $0.12 per kWh, the net profit from the system would be ~$284 in the first month. The predicted income in six months would be ~$750. However, this predication is very unreliable as the price is not stable and can change significantly.

As I said before, the calculation of earnings is dependent on the price of ETH and block difficulty. As of March 2017, the price of Ether broke past records and soared above $20, and on March 14, 2017, the price of Ether was $29.57 and the highest average difficulty, 180.235 TH, was recorded on 13 March. So according to the Ethereum profit calculator, the profit in the first month would have been $187, excluding the power costs. Despite the unbelievable increase in the Ether price, the earnings didn't increase proportionately because more miners went online and the earned Ethers were divided among the increased number of miners.

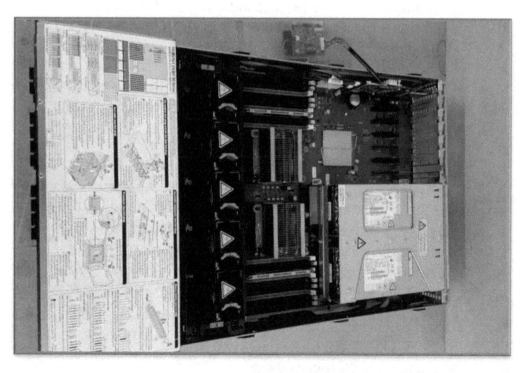

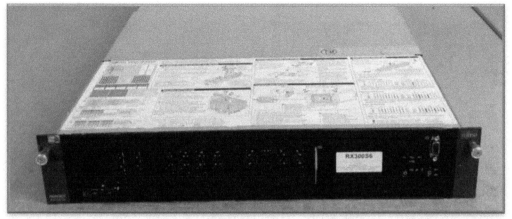

Figure 17 - Fujitsu PRIMERGY RX300 S6, with a pair of Xeon L5630 CPUs and 8 GB DDR3 ECC RAM

5.2.7. GPU-miner based on AMD Ryzen platform

Ryzen is the name of new CPU models by AMD which have been introduced in 2017. They are based on Zen microarchitecture. Ryzen supports PCIE 3.0, DDR4 memory and USB 3.1 natively. Ryzen is planned to come in three distinctive categories. Ryzen 7 is aimed at PC enthusiasts and people who use computers with a heavy workload. Ryzen 5 has four different CPUs, which may have four or six cores. The cheapest Ryzen 5 CPU is Ryzen 1400, the price of which is set at $169 MSRP[16]. It has four cores and 8 threads. The details of Ryzen 3 have not yet been published but should be available in the second quarter of 2017. Remember, the aim for the total cost of the motherboard, CPU and RAM combo is about $100–$125. If you spend more than $125 you will be wasting your money, unless these components can lead to a substantial reduction in the amount of power you use. However, this is unlikely to happen as the system CPU in a GPU mining rig stays idle for most of the time. So, always compare the idle power consumption of the whole CPU-motherboard-RAM combination.

As a GPU mining rig doesn't need a powerful CPU, the choice with Ryzen would be for the less powerful chipset of all. However, all the Ryzen CPU family use the AM4 socket made by AMD. While there are different AMD AM4 motherboards, you should seek for the cheapest that have the maximum number of PCIE slots. The best motherboard for a GPU mining rig is "ASRock AB350 GAMING K4". As it is displayed in picture below, this motherboard has six available PCIE slots and currently is priced at $110–120.

---

[16] MSRP is the list price, also known as the manufacturer's suggested retail price (MSRP).

However, the system may not be stable with six GPUs, as the motherboard is not designed for using all of PCIE slots at the same time for a heavy mining operation.

The recommended amount of RAM is 8 or 16 GB. The speed of RAM is not important, just try to find a cheap and reliable one. My recommendation is the 8 GB one of Crucial Ballistix Sport LT Single DDR4 2400, which is shows in picture below, and it is priced ~$50–$60.

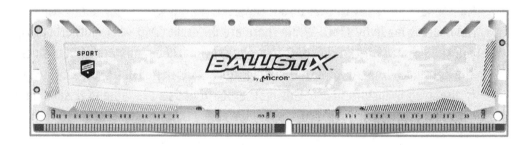

As the Ryzen motherboards come with M.2 storage slots, you do not need to have a SATA3-type storage. You can continue to use a M.2 SSD to minimize the system complexities. Again, I should say that the storage size should be based on the type of mining operation that you intend to undertake. For pooled mining, you do not need more than 128 GB of storage. Also, speed is not important. The crucial factor is the reliability of the storage. My recommendation is the SanDisk X400 128GB M.2 SSD which is priced at ~$60.

5.2.8. Building a professional mining farm

At the professional level, first you need to plan completely what you are going to do. You will need a substantial amount of money, time and patience. I have already discussed many of the financial points in Chapter 4. So, before you start building a GPU mining farm, you should review the previous chapters. You need the following to build a mining farm:

1. Many 6-GPU mining rigs.
2. A vacant space, a covered room, warehouse or building.
3. An industrial electrical power supply with the ability to provide 1000 watts to each mining rig.
4. Electrical connections and convertors, if required, for example, to convert 380 volts to 220 volts, as you are going to provide power to many mining rigs.
5. A stable internet connection and a mobile backup in case the link to the internet becomes interrupted.
6. Proper ventilation, and, if you plan to reroute the heated air outside or into another part of the building, air ducts or an air channel.
7. Physical security, as your mining farm is valuable and must be well protected against outside intrusions, requires care, control and maintenance.
8. Firefighting equipment, as the farm will run hot especially in the summer.
9. Maintenance, as cannot leave the farm alone for a long time without care and maintenance.

The figure below shows the basic structure of a mining farm.

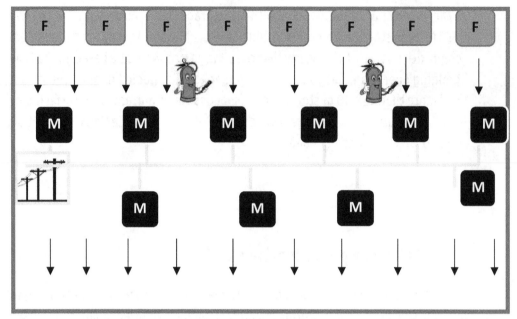

Figure 19 – A mining farm with 10-GPU miners, with only an incoming forced-air stream. M stands for miner, and F for fan.

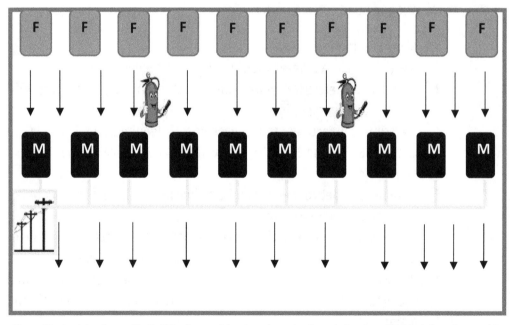

Figure 20 – A mining farm with 10-GPU miners, with only an incoming forced-air stream. M stands for miner, and F for fan.

What can we learn from these simple schematics?

1. Rectangular rooms are more suitable for mining rigs, as you need to place them in series next to each other in order to obtain the best arrangement for the removal of the generated heat.
2. If the room is square, or the heat from a mining rig would unduly affect an adjacent rig, you will need to design an independent air delivery system with channels for each miner, or an exhaust channel for each miner.
3. A 3-dimensional ventilation system, which delivers fresh air from the bottom of the floor and exhausts it through the ceiling, would be most appropriate. Although this might be regarded as an old-fashion way of ventilating, it is consistent with the fact that hot air rises.

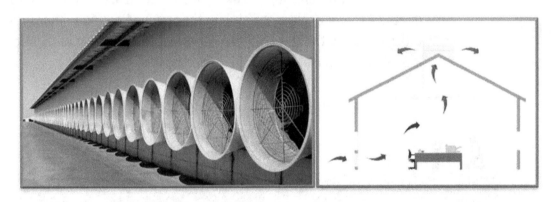

Figure 21 - This is a picture of a warehouse with many exhaust fans, located at the top of the wall close to the ceiling, reference is here!

4. You will need to plan your electrical line carefully as each of your mining rigs is worth more than $2000 and requires 1000 watts of uninterrupted power line (~5 amps from a 220-V system, or ~10 amps from a 110-V system). I have no expertise in electrical wiring systems, or how to wire your entire workplace, but there are many DIY articles that may help (some of the references are [11], [12], and [13]). However, work with an electrical system can be extremely dangerous and requires skill and expertise; never attempt to undertake it without proper knowledge [14][17]. The best way would be for you to design the layout yourself and then hire someone or a company to refine, and later, to implement it for you.

[17] Read more about electrical safety and hazards on "Canadian Centre for Occupational Health and Safety" website here!

From experience, I recommend that you use 120–150 CFM of air supply for each GPU. A 6-GPU mining rig therefore requires 720–900 CFM of air supply. You may see some mining rigs without external cooling fans, but as I said earlier, many problems can arise when you don't use cooling in addition to that provided by the fans of the GPUs. The reasons are:

1. GPUs run hot with only their own fans and can easily reach temperatures of 85–90° C under mining load.
2. When a GPU runs hot, its performance will reduce; a cold RX 470 can mine about ~24 MH/s, but one at 85° C can mine ~20 MH/s, i.e., a 20% reduction in performance.
3. When a GPU runs only with its own fans, an open-air style cooler (read more in Chapter 2) blows the air into the surroundings. In a mining rig with many GPUs, this may affect the performance of the other cards. Also, it creates a hot region around the mining rig.

Figure 22 - Example of an open-air style GPU cooler. Air is sucked in from front of the card and exhausted from in many directions.

4. When a card runs at a temperature higher than 80° C, the life of the GPU will be reduced exponentially (read more in Chapter 3). The ideal temperature for the GPU cores of a mining rig is below 80° C. I have not yet seen from any manufacturer a card that works below 80° C with its own GPU fans (this is with air rather than water cooling) when you run a heavy graphics benchmark like furmark software [15] or under a GPU mining load. You will need external cooling fans and some GPU

optimization with software such as "MSI Afterburner" in Windows OS to let GPU cooling fans run at higher speeds.

You can provide the recommended airflow of 720 CFM for each 6-GPU mining rig with twelve F12 Arctic PWM fans. These will cost less than $100. Computer fans require holders or fixing mounts, which will increase the cost a bit. My recommended expenditure on extra cooling ventilation for the whole system is 5–10% of the total cost of the mining rig. So, with our example system of a 6-GPU miner "Ex06-1150-Rev01" with a cost of ~$1900, an expenditure of $95–190 is recommended. Spending more than 10% of the total cost of a mining farm on a ventilation system is a waste of money. As said earlier, the target temperature for GPU core is 80° C or below. If the GPUs were to be water-cooled and they work at around 60° C under a mining load, you might overclock the system and obtain a further 5% or 10% gain but not more. So, use of water cooling does not improve things significantly and therefore isn't worth the extra cost.

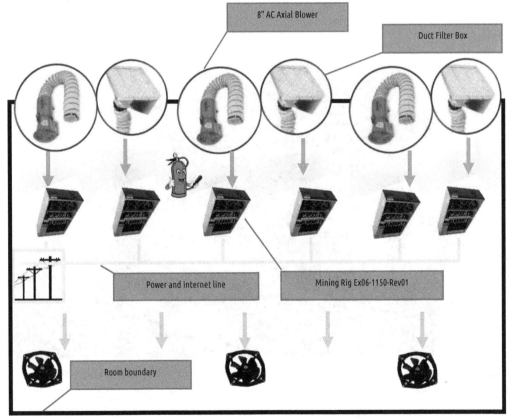

Figure 23 - This is a simple layout of a GPU mining farm with 6 units of "Ex06-1150-Rev01" (6 GPUs mining rig, link to the duct filter and axial fan are _here_!

Figure 24 - Picture of a well-organized mining farm with power of ~ 3000-4000 MH/s

Figure 25 - Picture of small mining farm of website: blockoperations.com, with about ten GPU mining rigs. Link is here!

Figure 26 - Picture of Genesis Mining farm: Enigma, one the world's largest Ethereum Mine, Link to the website is here!

5.2.9. Using water-cooled GPUs? Is it worth it?

In a test, GPU mining rig (see pictures below), I used a couple of the black edition of the XFX RX 480 8GB Reference design and have water cooled them with Thermaltake 3.0 CPU blocks, an external fan and a 240-mm radiator. The water-cooling system cost about ~€150, so if you buy the GPUs for ~$250–$280, the cost would be about 25% of the total cost of the GPUs. I do not recommend combining more than one GPU with the same water-cooling loop as the heat from the first will affect the other ones. You may pair two GPUs in one loop, but I have not tried to put three or four of them in a loop with a higher-flow pump or bigger radiator.

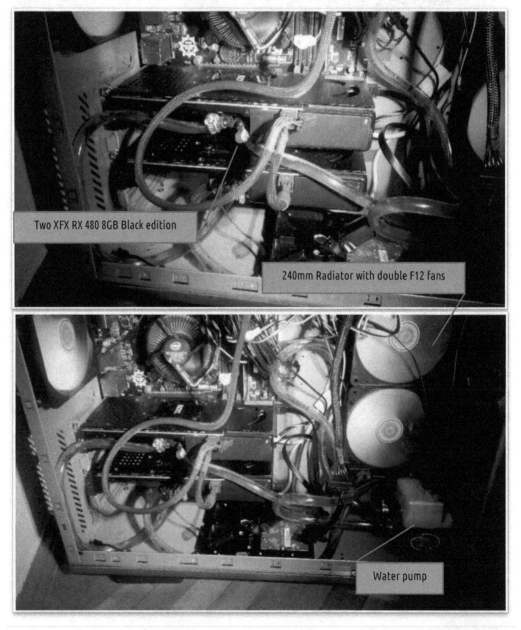

Two XFX RX 480 8GB Black edition

240mm Radiator with double F12 fans

Water pump

What are the advantages of a mining rig with water-cooled GPUs?

1. Obviously, the GPUs will run much cooler. In my system, the GPU0 temperature was ~55–60° C and the GPU1 temperature was ~65–70° C. So, the improvement over the system with an air-cooled GPU is a decrease of 10–15° C. Consequently, the stability of the system is at a maximum and the life of the GPU is prolonged.

2. At lower temperatures, your card will run at a maximum boost clock frequency which in my case was 1288 MHz. What about overclocking? As I said earlier, the AMD Radeon RX 400s series does not overclock very much; the maximum clock I could gain was 1345 MHz and at this frequency, I could not continue mining as the system crashed many times and I had to revert to its original boost clock. Overclocking the GPU core will make the GPU very unstable and the graphic card will crash or freeze more often. I have seen in some online threads[18] that a core clock close to 1400 MHz can be achieved with an over-voltage with the Radeon RX 480 8GB. However, as I explained earlier, if this extra 5%-10% gain in GPU performance in core clock frequency means that the system becomes more unstable and leads to the system crashing, then there is no benefit from overclocking. In other hand, overclocking has a risk of instability of the system which is not worth to take in a mining rig while a GPU mining rig is an unattended computer machine, must run very stable.

3. Water-cooled systems can be operated more quietly because the fans usually run at lower speeds than those of an air-cooled system.

4. If it is installed properly with a long tube and a strong pump, you can vent the heat to the outside or other designated place and the radiator can be mounted outside or in a colder place. The mining rig and radiator with fans should not be in a same compartment.

What are the disadvantages of a mining rig with water-cooled GPUs?

1. Obviously, there is the extra cost. A full water-cooling system could increase the cost of the mining rig by up to 30%—based on the cost of the water-cooling components, a complete water-block, a premium pump and fitting.

---

[18] According to Wikipedia "conversation threading is a feature used by many email clients, bulletin boards, newsgroups, and Internet forums in which the software aids the user by visually grouping messages with their replies."

2. You would inherit all of the problems of a customized water-cooled system, such as leakage and pump breakdown. Furthermore, installing the water-cooling unit itself requires skill and computer knowledge.
3. The biggest problem however is that in most cases, you would lose your warranty status if you disconnect the heatsink from the GPU chipset, as most manufacturers seal the screws that unblock the heatsink. It is totally not recommended to void the **warranty**.

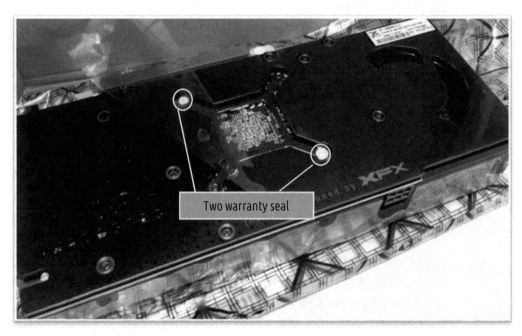

Figure 27 - Picture of the back of the black edition of the XFX RX 480 8GB reference design cooler. There are two warranty seals on the back of the card, protecting the heatsink of the GPU chip that would need to be unscrewed.

5.3. All about the mining-rig additional components and accessories

In Chapter 2, I briefly discussed the computer hardware that we use in a GPU mining rig. I should mention some of them again here but in more detail. In a complete mining rig with 5 GPUs, we would have PCIE-riser cards, many cooling fans, and a custom-made chassis for the rig. I will discuss these in turn.

5.3.1. PCIE-riser cards

Why do you need a PCIE-riser card? The answer is in order to connect the GPUs to the motherboard. Imagine that in the mining motherboard of "Asrock H81 Pro BTC", there is one slot for PCIE X16 and five slots for PCIE X1. As the GPUs only come with PCIE X16 sizes, you will need an adaptor to convert the PCIE X16 to the PCIE X1 of the motherboard.

Figure 28 - Asrock H81 Pro BTC with five units of PowerColor Rx 470 RedDevil edition

Most modern DDR3 and DDR4 motherboards, which offer PCIE 2nd generation X1 slots, have a bandwidth of 500 MB/s [16]. In the 1st of generation of PCIE X1, the speed was 250 MB/s. However, apparently, the GPU mining application doesn't saturate the whole bandwidth of the PCIE X1 slot, unlike a 3D game that may require a higher transfer rate[19].

There are many different types of PCIE-riser cards on the market, but in my opinion, the PCIE-raiser card of X1 to X16, which can be connected through a USB3 cable and powered board is the best and cheapest. It is usually priced around $10 and can be found easily in any electronic online shops. I usually get mine from Amazon through link below [17].

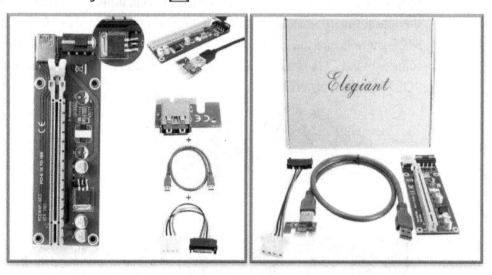

Here is another example of these PCIE-riser cards from a company called "mintcell" which are available on Amazon.com at this link.

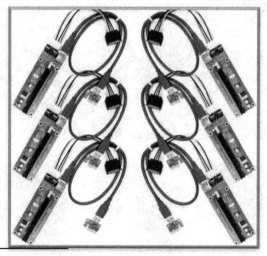

---

[19] Unfortunately, I have not found any particular software or tool to measure the PCIE-usage bandwidth to demonstrate here. I can only report on my personal experience.

The PCIE X1 card does not fix to the motherboard firmly and therefore when you work with a compact system, it may get lose or fall out of the socket. To prevent this, I usually fix them firmly with a hot glue once I have set up the system. This is not a very good solution if you decide that you want to remove them later on, as you may damage the slot. So, you should use just a little glue to keep the PCIE-riser card in place. Be verycareful not to damage your motherboard.

Figure 29 - Asrock Z97 Anniversary edition, 3 PCIE X1-riser cards being glued with hot glue gun.

Figure 30 - PCIE-riser cards are fixed by small amount of hot glue on the two button corners of the cards.

Figure 31 – A closer look at how I fixed the PCIE-riser card in the X1 PCIE slot with the hot glue.

After introduction of M.2 expansion slots and being a norm to implement it on every motherboard, companies have started to make relative accessories and possible adaptors. Related to the GPU mining rig is PCI Express 4X Female to NGFF M.2 M Key Male Adapter converter card that comes with power cable. This expansion card is being used to connect an extra GPU through M.2 expansion slot. So, a normal USB3 PCIE riser card is installed on the expansion card. As a result, a motherboard with 6 available PCIE slots can connect one or two more GPUs through M.2 port.

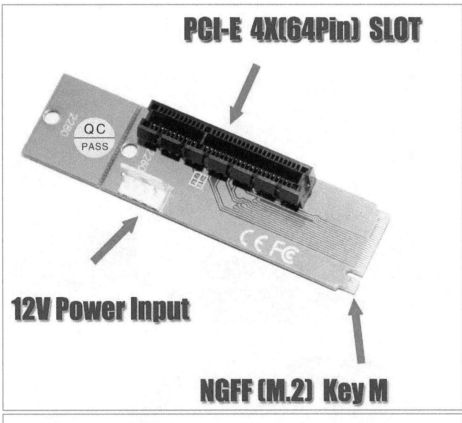

5.3.2. Remote control

The main problem with un-attended and remotely supervised GPU mining rig is the difficulty of restarting the system physically when system is frozen or crashed, as system becomes unresponsive and most of the time the resetting the system through software is not possible. However, there are few options available for such a problem, one of the is SSRv1 device, which is remotely controlled re-setter that can be connected to eight mining rigs at the same time and control the reset and power switch of the motherboard of the mining rig by wire. So, it can automatically reset frozen and crashed rigs. This device is available to buy on simplemining.net.

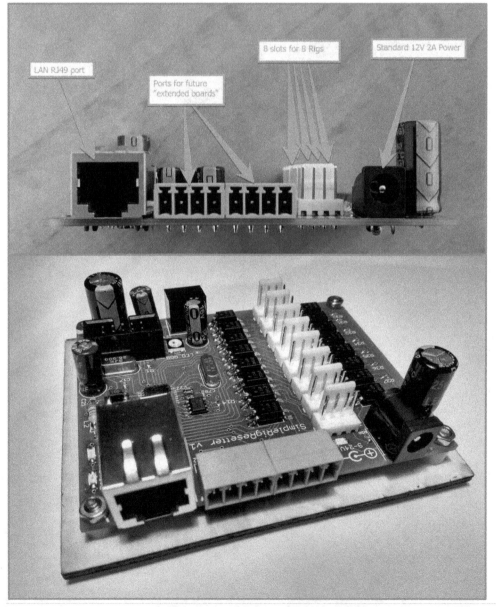

5.3.3. Cooling fans

Why do you need additional cooling fans? The reason is because the GPU itself does not deliver fresh air into the chassis. Usually a computer case is equipped with fans that bring fresh air into the system or exhaust the warm air to the outside. What about a mining rig? If you decide to have a maximum of 2 or 3 GPUs and you have placed in them in a typical full-tower ATX case, you require a very good air flow to keep them cool.

General information on computer-cooling fans is given in Chapter 2. Here I make a choice between the thousands of options that are out there, based on the following:

1. Fan noise, 2. Fan price, 3. Fan air flow, 4. Fan controllability

In my own builds, I go for affordable PWM fans which also have decent air flows. My recommended fan choices are:

ARCTIC F12 PWM PST- Standard Low Noise. They have a maximum airflow of 74 CFM (126 m³/h) and can be purchased for €5.99 [18]. These fans are very quiet and their price is almost half of that of the nearest competitor. In addition, being a PWM fan, it can be controlled much more easily by the motherboard. Also, the other unique characteristic is that they can be bonded together with a PST (PWM-Sharing Technology), so you wouldn't need many fan headers on the motherboard or an external fan controller. However, strangely, Arctic recently lowered the airflow of its F12 fans to 53 CFM (90.1 m³/h), see their website.

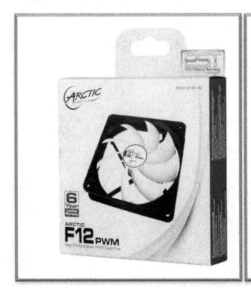

Each GPU usually requires **two** 120-mm-case fans for additional airflow in a mining-rig chassis.

What about your open-air chassis? If your rig has more than 2 GPUs, for instance 5 GPUs, and you have a custom-made chassis, you will require a higher airflow, which is hard to obtain with the computer-case fan. You need an airflow of 120–150 CFM per GPU to keep them sufficiently cool and under control.

My first choice is the 150-mm 220 V (or 110 V in USA) low-noise duct fan. I recommend these fans because:

1. Duct axial fans have less noise than the blow-type fans; the hub and shroud of the fan help the airflow pass more quietly.

2. 150 mm is the best size, as it has big enough blades for a decent airflow and also you can purchase 150-mm-diameter air ducts to route the air into and out of the system. In a closed-air system, or a computer-case type GPU mining rig, without air ducting, the airflow cannot be guided actively into and out of the system, as the system sucks in the air of the room and dumps the hot exhaust into the same atmosphere. But, with an air duct, you can bring fresh air from outside, insert a dust or humidity absorber on the way and then exhaust the warm air out of the room, or you can reuse the warm air for general purpose heating.

3. As I have already said, it is relatively cheap. I have purchased them for less than €20 [19] which is comparable to the price of a 120-mm-PWM fan! Each of these 150-mm fans has a maximum airflow of 257 CFM, but the actual airflow varies from manufacturer to manufacturer and you will need to study the product details before you purchase them. Always look for airflow and noise! <u>The noise should not be more 40–45 dB (A) (3m).</u>

So, for a five-GPUs system, you require ten PWM 120-mm-computer fans or three 150-mm-duct fans.

If you don't care about noise, and your cooling fans are being controlled by direct 12-V current or a fan controller that supply 12 volts, you should choose a high-RPM high-airflow fan. A good example is the Delta AFB1212VHE (link is here! And here!). A brushless 12-V fan with a current of 0.9 amps and a speed of 4000 RPM, should be able to deliver a maximum airflow of 129.9 CFM, which is almost twice that of the Arctic F12, with a noise level is 48 dB[20].

If you are looking for higher airflow and the noise of the fan is not important and you have a fan controller which is able to supply a 12-V, 4-A current to a fan header, you should go for a higher-grade PWM fan, such as **Delta TFC1212DE-SP07**. This can rotate at speeds of up to 5200 RPM and supply an airflow of 250 CFM with a current of 3.9 A. Here is the purchase link.

---

[20] Warning: do not connect these high-power fans to the motherboard fan headers, as the high wattage of the fan may damage the fan connectors.

Table 1 - This table shows the specification of high-airflow Delta fans. For more information, please visit delta-fan.com at this link! Pay attention to the CFM/Power columns, the higher numbers are better. The lower CFM fans have almost twice the efficiency than very high CFM fans.

Fan Part #	Size	Voltage Range	Voltage	Current (A)	Power(Watts)	Max RPM	Noise	Airflow (CFM)	CFM/Watt
PFR1212DHE	120x120x38	8.0~13.2	12V	3.7	44.4	7400	68.5	254	5.73
PFB1212UHE	120x120x38	8.0~13.2	12V	4	48	5500	66.5	253	5.27
AFB1212GHE-C	120x120x38	6.0~13.8	12V	2.45	29.4	5200	62	241	8.20
PFR1212UHE	120x120x38	8.0~13.2	12V	2.7	32.4	6600	65.5	229	7.06
PFB1212GHE	120x120x38	8.0~13.2	12V	2.7	32.4	4800	64	218	6.72
AFB1212EHE-C	120x120x38	6.0~13.8	12V	1.8	21.6	4600	58.5	213	9.84
QFR1212GHEXUM	120x120x38	8 ~ 13.2	12V	1.8	21.6	6000	64	210	9.74
AFB1212EHF	120x120x32	6.0~12.6	12V	1.85	22.2	4800	59	199	8.95
AFB1212SHE-C	120x120x38	6.0~13.8	12V	1.25	15	4100	55.5	190	12.70
FFB1212EHE	120x120x38	7.0~13.2	12V	2	24	4000	59	190	7.92
THB1212B-AXHF	120x120x25	7.0~15.0	12V	1.6	19.2	5300	59	184	9.59
PFB1212EHE	120x120x38	8.0~13.2	12V	1.6	19.2	4000	59	181	9.44
FFB1212SHE	120x120x38	7.0~13.2	12V	1.5	18	3600	56.5	171	9.50
AFB1212SHE	120x120x38	4.0~13.2	12V	1.05	12.6	3700	53	152	12.05
FFB1212VHE	120x120x38	7.0~13.2	12V	1	12	3200	53	152	12.65

What are the other options? You can always go for a simple blower axial-style fans, but I'm not keen on these. They are however easier to place next to the rig, and they work well when the room has an exhaust fan or ventilation, as a blow-style fan just blows the hot air away from the system into the surrounding environment. However, you can't do anything about filtering the air. Furthermore, you don't want to spend a lot on cooling units that have a low efficiency and consume a lot of power. Always look at the price, airflow and power consumption. The fan below from "Trotec" or similar types seem to be good options if you want to use this type of fan [19].

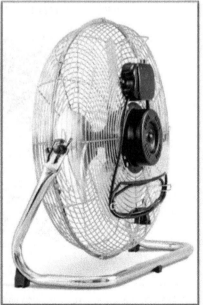

As explained at the end of Chapter 2, the recommended fan type for a GPU mining-rig is an airflow-optimized fan, not a static-pressure-optimized fan. In a open-air chassis style, there is no restriction or obstacles such as a radiator or dust filter in the way of the stream of air. The purpose of an external fan on a GPU mining rig is to exhaust the warm air of the GPUs out of the system. So, the main feature of an efficient axial fan is to bring a high airflow the system.

Always look at the fan efficiency. Do the calculation for yourself, as follows:

The efficiency (Eff) of a simple fan of a GPU mining rig is given by the formula:

Eff = maximum airflow rate (CFM)/ (maximum power of fan in W)

Accordingly, the points below should be considered:

1. The maximum airflow rate of a fan should be more than 70 CFM.
2. The maximum power of a fan is with the voltage (12 V) multiplied by the maximum current (A).
3. **An** efficiency (Eff) of more than 12 is acceptable.

Why is fan efficiency so important? Imagine this scenario: your AMD Radeon RX 470 consumes around ~120 watthours, and suppose that you need an extra air stream of 150 CFM to maintain the recommended airflow to a GPU. While this airflow can be delivered with an efficient 120-mm fan such as "Delta FFB1212VHE", this extra airflow requires 12 watts of energy, which is 10% of the total GPU consumption. consequently, considering the cost of power, the efficiency of the fan is important. Note that some AC fans have terrible airflow efficiencies. So, you should give careful consideration to the choice of fans.

The efficiency (Eff) of the ARCTIC F12 PWM PST is given by:

Eff = 53 / (0.24 x 12) = 18.75

where 53 is the maximum flowrate (CFM)[21], 0.24 is the current (A) and 12 is the voltage.

Another competitor is the "Noctua NF-S12B [20] redux-1200 PWM" which is currently priced at ~€12–14 on Amazon. Noctua is a computer hardware manufacturer of CPU coolers and computer fans for primarily the enthusiast market [21]. Noctua has many different designs and types of fans, but other the

---

[21] Recently Arctic lowered the airflow of F12 fans to 53 CFM (90.1 m³/h), see their website.

important of the cooling system is: its costs, most of Noctua fans are expensive and are targeted for premium and enthusiastic customers.

So, let's calculate the efficiency (Eff) of the Noctua NF-S12B fan:

Eff = 59 / 0.9 = 65, where 59 is the maximum flowrate (CFM) and 0.9 is the power.

5.3.4. The complete HVAC[22] system

As I said in the previous section, you can't get away with just a few simple blowers or a couple of exhaust-duct fans. You will require a complete operative HVAC system in your mining farm. Ventilation and air conditioning are important matters that need to be taken into account in the design of a building or room for a GPU mining farm. I don't intend to get into this. Suffice it to say that before you decide to carry on with your GPU mining-rig plans, you will need to think ahead, and in doing this, you should take account of the following:

1. How big is your mining farm? Typically, you will require about 5 square-meters for each mining rig with 6 GPUs. For horizontal ventilation, a rectangular-shaped room would be better with a length/width ratio greater than 2. For vertical ventilation, the room should be high enough to allow the heat to be collected and vented

---

[22] Heating, ventilation and air conditioning

to the outside. So, four 6-GPU miners will need a 20-square-meter room, preferably ~6.5 m by ~3 m.

2. You require at least 100 CFM of extra airflow for each GPU than is provided by the GPU fans themselves (I recommended a total of about 720 CFM for a 6-GPU mining rig above). So, for four 6-GPU miners (i.e. with a total of 24 GPUs), you will require a ventilation of 24 x 100 CFM, i.e. 2400 CFM. You may think this is overkill, but definitely you will need it on hot summer days. If you don't spend money on good ventilation, you will pay later by reducing the life of the components or lowering the performance of the GPUs.

3. You will need to filter out the dust before it reaches the mining farm. Also, the fresh air may be humid, in which case, you will need to deal with both dust and humidity. Think carefully about the choice of location.

4. What's your plan for the generated heat? In the previous four-miner-example case, you would have been generating about 4000 watts of heat. You can reuse and circulate it in the building or just dump it outside.

A simple schematic of a ventilation system for a mining farm is given in Chapter 4 (where a more than five 6-GPU mining rig is available) consists of:

1. An air inlet.
2. An air box, air-inlet filter, or inline filter (different names for the same component).
3. A duct fan.
4. Duct and air channels.
5. A blower, axial fan.
6. An exhaust air collector.
7. An air outlet with exhaust fan.
8. A temperature monitor and controller.

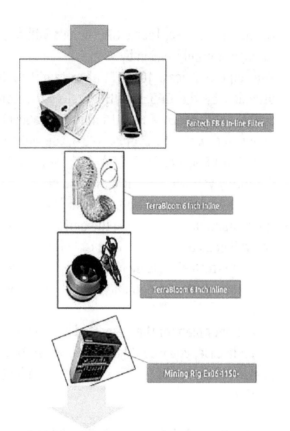

But you will need to remember that expenditure on a ventilation system should not exceed the suggested budget of 5%–10% of the total cost of the mining rig.

5.3.5. Dust filtration

In general conditions, you can use a simple PVC computer-fan grill or air filter to filter out the dust. These can be bought from your electrical hardware shop in 120-mm or 140-mm sizes, with pack of 10 costing about $10 [22]. They can be mounted in front of the intake fans and should be cleaned from time to time. These filters are easy to fix to any mining rig.

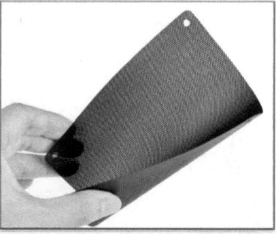

However, in a professional mining farm which has many open-air chassis GPU miners, it is not possible to use a simple dust filter as the external cooling is carried out using high-airflow blower fans or duct fans.

If the place doesn't have a central HVAC system, such as an empty room or warehouse, you can choose an easier solution. Select enough suction fans and attach them to the designated filters.

Figure 32 - Here is an example of a cheap 6" 442 CFM Ducting Inline Fan Blower with duct and filter. Link is here!

Duct fans are not suitable for blowing air into the mining rig. If you plan to use only duct fans, you will require to:

1. Place the intake-duct fans with filters to suck in fresh air.
2. Design and build proper air channels and ducts, ensuring that the air stream is passing through all of the mining rigs.
3. Place the exhaust-duct fans to push out the warm air.

As I said earlier, the design, implementation and installation of a ventilation system isn't simple and requires knowledge, skill and tools. However, to make it work while not costing too much, you will need to study, breakdown the job into simple steps, start from an easy plan and then improve it by trial and error.

At the beginning, try to start with one blower fan for each mining rig and a few exhaust fans to remove the heat from the room. Dust won't be a problem for the mining rig in the short term—you can fix that later. After that, try to improve the air quality by adding air filters to the incoming air, make simple air channels to feed each miner individually, check the running temperatures and **finally** add more blowers if necessary. Always think ahead—on a summer's day with the ambient temperature above 30° C, your system may get crippled.

5.4. The mining software on a GPU mining rig

Your mining rig must have an operating system capable of running mining software. Two options are available: Windows and Linux. The choice of mining software depends on how you have decided to do the mining, whether to run the rig in a mining pool or solo. Here we discuss the options.

5.4.1. Operating systems

1. Windows

Well, most non-professional GPU mining rigs (rigs not operating a large-scale mining farm) run on the Windows 7 operating system. Why?

1. It is easy to set up the whole system: 1. to install OS; 2. to install the required system and GPU drivers; 3. to set up and run the mining software; 4. to monitor and tweak the system configuration, for instance, to change the fan speed. The Linux operating system requires a lot of computer knowledge. There are always problems related to incompatibility of hardware. These problems start with installing Linux itself, regardless of version, making a bootable USB, and, later on, installing the GPU drivers, as AMD drivers are not available for all Linux variants. Recently, AMD released a driver for the AMD RX series for Ubuntu 16.04, which is one of most famous revisions of Linux.

2. It is compatible with mining software. Some mining applications do not work efficiently enough with Windows 10, due to incompatibility.

3. It is relatively cheap. At the moment, it costs ~$100 but it can be found in some software discount online shops for much less. Even $100 is a reasonable price to pay for a $2000-mining rig.

However, purchasing a new Windows licence even for $20 would not be appropriate for a low-budget build. As I said regarding the budget-build GPU mining rigs, it is always better to buy an old working computer with storage and a genuine and activated Windows OS. You should be able to buy a whole computer, with an installed OS, for less than $100. This is still a viable option as most of the full-size ATX desktop computers (not micro-ATX size) have 4-PCIE slots available and by tweaking the PSU, you should be able to convert it to a decent mining rig (please read more on this in the Chapter on mining-rig build options based on budget).

2.   Linux

According to linux.com, Linux has evolved into one of the most reliable computer ecosystems on the planet. Combine that reliability with zero cost of entry and you have the perfect solution for a desktop platform. Linux is also distributed under an open-source license. Linux has a number of different versions to suit nearly any type of user. From new users to hard-core users, you'll find a "flavor" of Linux to match your needs. These versions are called "distributions" (or, in the short form, "distros"). Nearly every distribution of Linux can be downloaded for free, burned onto a disk (or USB thumb drive), and installed (on as many machines as you like). The most popular Linux distributions are: Ubuntu Linux, Linux Mint, Arch Linux, Deepin, Fedora, Debian, CentOs [23].

What is the best Linux flavor for a GPU mining rig? It really doesn't matter what distribution you use, as most of them do not have much influence on the execution of the mining software. The most important matter is the AMD driver for your GPU. The best mining GPU of 2017, the Radeon RX 400 Series of AMD RX 470 4GB, requires an AMDGPU-PRO Driver for Linux to function [24]. At the moment, AMD is compatible with RedHat Enterprise Linux® 7.3 (64-bit version), RedHat Enterprise Linux® 6.8 (64-bit version), Ubuntu 16.04 (64-bit version), CentOS 7.3 (64-bit version), CentOS 6.8 (64-bit version), SLED/SLES 12 SP2 (64-bit version) distributions, but this may change with time. Installing the AMD driver on one of the Linux distributions, which I have not mentioned here, is not difficult and can be done with some tweaks.

But one word of warning. In the past, I have built numerous desktop machines, but never could I could install a Linux OS with the GPU drivers on a desktop without a lot of difficulty, including searching on the internet for solutions. If you are not familiar with Linux systems, or are not a software expert and don't know a lot about programming and scripting, do not enter the Linux world; just carry on using Windows. However, as access to the software is free and easy, you can always try it out, when you have time and a computer to experiments with it. **Always remember:** 1. first install Linux OS without any GPU cards installed. If you are using an intel-based CPU, just use your IGP (Integrated Graphics Processor) to complete the installation; 2. then add your GPUs using PCIE-riser cards, and 3. then install the GPU drivers.

Here are some of the tips that may help you in setting up a Linux OS-based GPU mining rig.

1. Download your free distribution of Linux OS. I recommend you go for Ubuntu 16.04.1 LTS [24], here is the link!
2. Make a bootable USB stick with "**Universal-USB-Installer**" [25], link is here! (there is a lot of guidance on the website that will help you make a bootable USB stick). I do not recommend other boot makers such as "**Rufus**" or "**ISO to USB**". While they don't work well with Linux OS ISO and images, most of the time you are confronted with errors during the installation such as "unable to find a medium containing a live file system".
3. Boot your computer with the USB stick and install the Ubuntu. It's pretty straightforward. If you need guidance, please refer to this link on the Ubuntu website.
4. When the installation is finished, you will need to update the Ubuntu software, through software updater, and then restart the Ubuntu.
5. Install your PCIE-riser cards and GPUs, and then turn the mining rig on.
6. Download and install the AMDGPU-PRO Driver for Ubuntu 16.04, Link is here! There is a simple guideline on how to install the driver on the AMD website here and also on the Ubuntu website here!
7. Also you require to install OpenCL software, according to AMD "OpenCL™ Accelerated Parallel Processing (APP) technology is a set of advanced hardware and software technologies that enable AMD graphics processing cores (GPU), working in concert with the system's x86 cores (CPU), to execute heterogeneously to accelerate many applications beyond just graphics.", where can be found on AMD website here!

As I said earlier, you might be faced with a lot of trouble in installing and running the AMD driver with the Linux OS and you may need to do a lot of reading and troubleshooting.

5.4.2. Solo mining or pooled mining

According to bitcoin wiki [26], solo mining is when a miner performs the mining operations alone without joining a pool. All mined blocks are generated to the miner's credit.

The website gives the pros and cons of solo and pooled mining. These are as follows:

Pros of pooled mining:

1. It generates a steadier income, and it has a low variance as you get paid every day.
2. It usually generates a higher income.
3. It is easy to setup and leaves most of the headaches with the pool admin(s).
4. It has extra features—pools usually let you quickly check the status of your miners from anywhere, and notify you of payouts and other matters, all of which would take you a lot of extra time to set up on your own.
5. It requires much less space—if you are solo mining, you need to keep your own copy of the blockchain, while pools handle all that by themselves.
6. It's very easy to switch between mining pools. Should one of them become irresponsive or not so profitable to operate, all you would need to do is just change the address of the mining pool and its related parameters on the mining software. Usually, this can be done in less than a minute.

Cons of pooled mining:

1. Pooled mining can suffer interruptions from outages at the pool provider. So, you would be relying on a third-party system to earn your money. Pool websites can go down, and when they do, your miners would be idling.

2. Pools are subject to DOS attacks and there can be other causes of downtimes. Backup pools and solo mining can be configured to deal with these situations.
3. Pooled mining generates a smaller income due to fees being charged and transaction fees not being cashed out. But since the middle of 2016, because of many new entrants to the Ethereum mining-pool network, the fees went down to around 1%–2%.
4. As stated in http://bitcoin.stackexchange.com, giving power to the pool owner, some important decisions regarding the future of Bitcoin are made by people voting with their blocks. Some time ago, the Bitcoin community had to choose between two BIPs that fulfilled the same role. The voting was done by the coinbase transactions containing a vote for either one of the BIPs. By giving their computing powers to the pools, the miners essentially gave their votes to pool owners to vote as they choose.

Pros of solo mining:

1. Solo mining is less prone to outages resulting in higher uptime.
2. It doesn't incur any fees. For each discovered block, the transaction fees are paid to the miner.

Cons of solo mining:

1. Solo mining tends to generate more erratic income.
2. Solo mining wastes a lot of time and requires the user to do a lot of searching solely in order to solve the network puzzle.
3. Complicated setup and start up as you are your own pool admin, assuming you have the technical skills necessary.

A solo miner who prefers to have full control over their Ethereum (ETH) addresses by running a local node with a full copy of the Ethereum blockchain, could soon start having free space issues as the storage requirements continue to grow at a rapid rate. The Ethereum blockchain data are already getting close to 30 GB in size and as Ethereum (ETH) and Ethereum Classic (ETC) have now separated, you may need to make a copy of both blockchains, and you would require another 30 GB of data for the ETC local wallet and blockchain [27]. To start mining, you would need to download the blockchain for Ethereum. At this point, you should be synchronizing with the rest of the Ethereum network. This can take a while depending on your internet speed and the current size of the blockchain—anywhere between 20 min and several hours [28].

What is Pooled Mining?

Pooled mining "pools" all the resources of the clients in that pool to generate the solution to a given block. When the pool solves a block, the reward generated by that block's solution is split and distributed between the pool's participants.

As Wikipedia adds "In the context of cryptocurrency mining, a mining pool is the pooling of resources by miners, who share their processing power over a network, to split the reward equally, according to the amount of work they contributed to solving a block. A "share" is awarded to members of the mining pool who present a valid proof of work (PoW) that their miner solved." [29]

To mine through a mining pool, you need to connect to the mining server and send your POW (proof of work, read more on Chapter 1). You will be rewarded according to your contribution to the mining process. The most important matter here is that the mining pool should be big and strong enough to have a good chance of solving the puzzle and get rewarded. Otherwise, it won't be able to pay for the shares which have been contributed by all the connected miners. There are several important factors to help you in choosing between mining pools. These are:

1. **The average hashrate of the mining pool** for the Ethereum network. The highest average hashrate of 7750.7955 GH/s was recorded on Thursday, January 19, 2017 [30]. Since January 2017 and the price of Ether has risen dramatically, from $12 to $48 in April 2017. The average network hashrate has also increased. The highest average hashrate of 17900.8160 GH/s was recorded on April 11, 2017. A big hashrate power for a mining pool is an advantage. The chart below shows the mining share of the big Ethereum miners. Again, there was a huge jump from ~$50 to ~$170!! at the end of May 2017. Highest average hashrate of 29819.2767 GH/s was recorded on Monday, May 22, 2017. Although the price has risen more 300%, the average hashrate did not increase at the same rate.

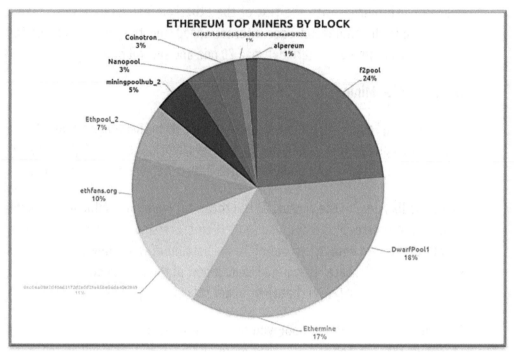

ETHEREUM TOP MINERS BY BLOCK

Figure 33 - Ethereum top miners by block, according to the Etherescan website, link is <u>here</u>!

2. **The reliability of the mining pool**. A server can go offline and interrupt the mining operation. There are no statistics to demonstrate the performance of a mining pool other than the total number of miners and the hashrate power of the pool. When you start your mining business, during the first month you may acquire a lot of experience on the pool performance and reliability. Always try to keep two mining-pool options available, so that when one goes offline or doesn't perform well, the other can be switched on.

3. **The payment methods**. Each mining pool has a fee and regulations on how to pay the miner's share. For instance, **my favorite mining pool, nanopool.org**, payments are executed 4 times a day and the current minimum payout is 0.2 ETH. The mining pool eth.pp.ua, says "the fee is 1% and a network fee is payable on withdrawal. It is once a day if your balance exceeds 0.1 Ether. We payout uncle[23] (orphan) block rewards!" [31]. Some mining pools have

---

[23] What is uncle block? Well it is little technical. Uncles are orphaned blocks that contribute to the security of the main chain, but are not considered the canonical "truth" for that particular chain height. Due to advances in blockchain research, it was shown that significantly lower block times were possible and perhaps beneficial given the current connectivity of the internet. One of the potential risks of a low block time is a higher rate of orphaned blocks (competing mined blocks that do not make it into the main chain). To counter this, a GHOST protocol is used which pays for these valid blocks, adding to the security of the main chain. Instead of the main chain being "longest", it is instead "heaviest". So, this matter helps rewarding miners for when duplicate block solutions are found because of the shorter block times of Ethereum (compared to other cryptocurrency). An uncle is a smaller reward than a full block. (And if they are submitted later than the next block, the reward rapidly diminishes, ending at zero after seven blocks later.)

different algorithms for payment and won't pay out until a block is found or your shared balanced exceeds a certain amount. You therefore would need to try several mining pools to determine which would be the most suitable for you. Based on your total hashrate power, choose one primary through which you mine and one secondary (reserved), which can be used when the first pool goes offline.

4. **The number of servers, and their locations**. Always mine with a pool that has a server close to your location. Big mining pools, such as Dwarfpool or Ethermine, have several servers in different locations around the world—in North America, Europe, Asia, China and Russian Federation. A close server has the advantage of having a lower ping and higher stability for regional use.

5. **The support, guidelines and services**. Some mining pools have a fantastic help section with good guidelines for beginners. A good example is **nanopool.org.** In the section, "Getting started", you will find the best step-by-step walk-through to start a mining business [32].

References

[1] Bitcoin Wiki, "Why a GPU Mines Faster than a CPU" [Online]. Available: https://en.bitcoin.it/wiki/Why_a_GPU_mines_faster_than_a_CPU. [Accessed: 15-Jan-2017].

[2] Tweaktown.com, 2013, "MSI Radeon R9 280X 3GB Twin Frozr OC in CrossFire Video Card Review," TweakTown [Online]. Available: http://www.tweaktown.com/reviews/5826/msi-radeon-r9-280x-3gb-twin-frozr-oc-in-crossfire-video-card-review/index23.html. [Accessed: 02-Jan-2017].

[3] PCWorld.com, 2016, "AMD Radeon RX 460 Review: An Affordable Graphics Card with Bleeding-Edge Tech," PCWorld [Online]. Available: http://www.pcworld.com/article/3104596/components-graphics/amd-radeon-rx-460-review-an-affordable-graphics-card-with-bleeding-edge-tech.html. [Accessed: 02-Jan-2017].

[4] Vmodtech.com, "AMD RADEON RX 480 3-Ways CROSSFIRE SHOWTIME."

[5] Fujitsu, "Datasheet of Fujitsu PRIMERGY TX300 S5 Server" [Online]. Available: https://sp.ts.fujitsu.com/dmsp/Publications/public/ds-py-tx300-s5-rh.pdf. [Accessed: 07-Jan-2017].

[6] servershop24.de, "FSC Primergy TX300 S5 Mainboard / System Board Socket 1366 - S26361-D2619-A14 GS3" [Online]. Available: https://www.servershop24.de/en/components/motherboards/fsc-primergy-tx300-s5-mainboard-system-board-socket-1366-s26361-d2619-a14-gs3/a-112305/. [Accessed: 07-Jan-2017].

[7] Fujitsu, "Fujitsu PRIMERGY RX300 S6 Dual Socket 2 U Rack Server" [Online]. Available: https://sp.ts.fujitsu.com/dmsp/Publications/public/ds-py-rx300-S6.pdf. [Accessed: 07-Jan-2017].

[8] servershop24.de, "Fujitsu Primergy RX300 S6, Server Mainboard / System Board - D2619-N15 GS1" [Online]. Available: https://www.servershop24.de/en/fujitsu-primergy-rx300-s6-server-mainboard-system-board-d2619-n15-gs1/a-114539/. [Accessed: 07-Jan-2017].

[9] Alphr, "Fujitsu Primergy RX300 S6 Review," Alphr [Online]. Available: http://alphr.com/servers/30955/fujitsu-primergy-rx300-s6-review. [Accessed: 07-Jan-2017].

[10] Intel, "Intel® Xeon® Processor 5000 Sequence," Intel® ARK Prod. Specs [Online]. Available: https://ark.intel.com/products/family/28144/Intel-Xeon-Processor-5000-Sequence. [Accessed: 07-Jan-2017].

[11] http://www.familyhandyman.com, "How to Wire a Garage (Unfinished)," Fam. Handyman [Online]. Available: http://www.familyhandyman.com/electrical/wiring/how-to-wire-a-garage-unfinished. [Accessed: 08-Jan-2017].

[12] http://www.diynetwork.com, "The Ultimate Workshop: Lighting and Electrical Layout," DIY [Online]. Available: http://www.diynetwork.com/how-to/skills-and-know-how/workshops/the-ultimate-workshop-lighting-and-electrical-layout. [Accessed: 08-Jan-2017].

[13] WOOD Magazine, 2016, "Critical Questions about Workshop Wiring," WOOD Mag. [Online]. Available: http://www.woodmagazine.com/woodworking-tips/techniques/outfitting-woodworking-shop/critical-questions-about-workshop-wiring. [Accessed: 08-Jan-2017].

[14] Government of Canada, C. C. for O. H. and S., 2017, "Electrical Safety - Basic Information: OSH Answers" [Online]. Available: https://www.ccohs.ca/oshanswers/safety_haz/electrical.html. [Accessed: 08-Jan-2017].

[15] oZone3D.Net, "FurMark: VGA Stress Test, Graphics Card and GPU Stability Test, Burn-in Test, OpenGL Benchmark and GPU Temperature |" [Online]. Available: http://www.ozone3d.net/benchmarks/fur/. [Accessed: 08-Jan-2017].

[16] Hardwaresecrets.com, 2012, "Everything You Need to Know About the PCI Express," Hardw. Secrets.

[17] Amazon.de, *ELEGIANT USB 3.0 PCI-E Express 1x Zu 16x Extender Riser Card Adapter Power Kable Mining*.

[18] Amazon.de, *ARCTIC F12 PWM Rev.2 - Standard Low Noise PWM Controlled Case Fan*.

[19] Amazon.de, *TROTEC Bodenventilator TVM 18 | 120 Watt Leistung | Durchmesser 45 Cm | 3 Geschwindigkeitsstufen | Chrom-Design | Inkl. Tragegriff*.

[20] noctua.at, "NF S12B Redux-1200 PWM SPECIFICATIONS" [Online]. Available: http://noctua.at/en/nf-s12b-redux-1200-pwm/specification. [Accessed: 02-Feb-2017].

[21] Wikipedia, the free encyclopedia, 2017, "Noctua (Company)," Wikipedia.

[22] Amazon.de, *eBoot 140 Mm PVC Black Computer PC Fan Fan Fan Fan Grill Dust Filter Filter Mat Case Pack of 10*.

[23] Linux, 2014, "How to Choose the Best Linux Desktop for You," Linuxcom Source Linux Inf. [Online]. Available: https://www.linux.com/learn/how-choose-best-linux-desktop-you. [Accessed: 18-Jan-2017].

[24] Ubuntu, "Install Ubuntu 16.04 LTS" [Online]. Available: https://www.ubuntu.com/download/desktop/install-ubuntu-desktop. [Accessed: 19-Jan-2017].

[25] pendrivelinux.com, 2010, "Universal USB Installer - Easy as 1 2 3," USB Pen Drive Linux [Online]. Available: https://www.pendrivelinux.com/universal-usb-installer-easy-as-1-2-3/. [Accessed: 19-Jan-2017].

[26] Bitcoin Wiki, "Pool vs. Solo Mining" [Online]. Available: https://en.bitcoin.it/wiki/Pool_vs._solo_mining. [Accessed: 19-Jan-2017].

[27] Crypto Mining Blog, "Ethereum Blockchain Size" [Online]. Available: http://cryptomining-blog.com/tag/ethereum-blockchain-size/. [Accessed: 19-Jan-2017].

[28] Ethereum Stack Exchange, "Blockchain - What Are the Ethereum Disk Space Needs?" [Online]. Available: http://ethereum.stackexchange.com/questions/143/what-are-the-ethereum-disk-space-needs. [Accessed: 14-Oct-2016].

[29] Wikipedia, the free encyclopedia, 2017, "Mining Pool," Wikipedia.

[30] Etherscan, "Ethereum Network HashRate Growth Chart" [Online]. Available: https://etherscan.io/chart/hashrate. [Accessed: 20-Jan-2017].

[31] eth.pp.ua, "Eth.pp.ua - Ethereum Mining Pool" [Online]. Available: https://eth.pp.ua/. [Accessed: 20-Jan-2017].

[32] Nanopool, "Help" [Online]. Available: https://etc.nanopool.org/help. [Accessed: 04-Feb-2017].

Chapter 6
A quick guide on building a GPU mining rig

6.1.How to start?

At this point, I will assume that you have a pretty good understanding of what is involved in GPU mining and how a GPU mining rig works. You should therefore be almost ready to start building your first GPU mining rig, or to improve an existing one. In this short chapter, I will summarize the information given in the previous chapters in the form of a step-by-step guide on how to build a GPU mining rig. In the final section of this chapter, I will give some updated buying tips related to building a GPU mining rig. The data are based on the market information available at the end of May 2017.

6.2.Define your goals and budget

It is very important that you first decide what you want to do, whether it Is your intention to try either to use or to mine cryptocurrency. If you are not sure, then I suggest you reread Chapter 5.

My aim here is only to provide guidance for those who intend to build a specialized computer for the purpose of mining cryptocurrency. The minimum budget of this is $1000 and maximum is $2000. This relates to the building of one GPU mining rig. You may, of course, decide to build several units.

6.3. Chassis design choice

The choice of chassis is the open-air style. Here you will need to decide whether to build or to buy a GPU mining rig chassis. The important point is that the chassis must be able to accommodate six GPUs. If you make the chassis yourself, you may be able to save up to $100, but most probably it won't be as neat as a ready-made one.

If you live in Europe, you can try to search for a chassis on your local eBay store, for instance, eBay.de, or search on Google for "GPU mining rig Europe".

One of the online stores in Europe can be found here: www.ethereumminer.eu .

The picture below shows one type of chassis design, which is called "SimpleXX Stack". Their website boasts that this is the best case/frame for your mining rig and this may well be the case. It is easy to build and with its open framework, you can add up to a maximum of six GPUs. In May 21, 2017, it cost €89.95 which is very reasonable, but you may have to pay for shipping, because the mining chassis is pretty heavy.

The other option in Europe is the online shop: www.mineshop.eu. You can buy a complete ready-to-plugin-and-work GPU mining rig or just buy the chassis and accessories. According to their website, the mining chassis is designed for building professional cryptocurrency mining rigs. It is very strong and the rig can be easily cooled. It also makes efficient use of space for professional mining rigs for both home and farms. It is light, being made of high-quality aluminum. In May 2017, the chassis cost about €77; the delivery cost from Ireland to Austria, my home country was €110,43.

In the United States, there are many options, from Amazon.com to eBay.com and many online webstores. Just search for "GPU mining rig" or "mining chassis" and you will find numerous buying options. Just remember not to spend more than $150 on the chassis alone. The ideal cost range including shipping charges for the chassis only is $100–$150.

Many of these chassis have been mentioned in Chapter 5. There is also the option of buying a chassis with PCIE riser cards and a suitable power supply. One of these chassis builders is Centrix International Corp. (www.centrix-intl.com) which also sells their products on eBay.com. Their chassis was priced at $274 in May 2017, and according to eBay it has already sold 74 units, which is a very impressive number. Furthermore, the seller has a 99.5% positive feedback on eBay.com. However, the chassis with a server PSU **does not have an ATX 24-pin motherboard output,** so you would require pairing your system with a low-wattage PSU to run your system. In this chassis, a HP server/workstation power supply is used and a power splitter is required to distribute the power among the GPUs. One of the favorite PSUs for mining rigs is HP DPS-1200FB A 1200W, which originally belonged to HP ProLiant DL580 G5 and similar computers. These kinds of PSU are very efficient with more than 90% efficiency under full load, and are built to endure a heavy workload and very stable.

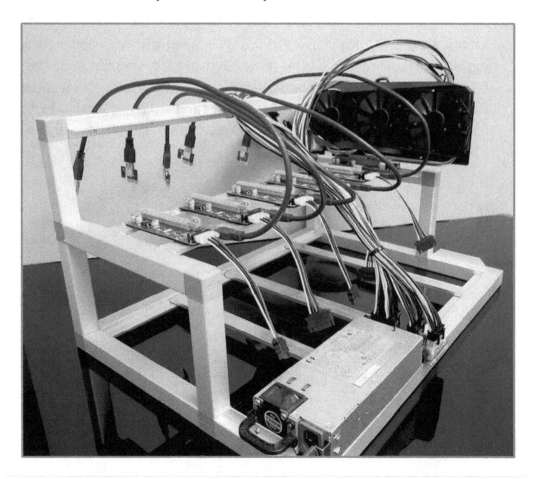

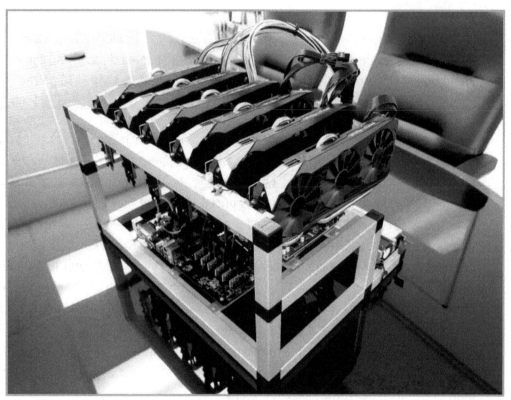

Figure 2 – Picture of a chassis from www.centrix-intl.com with six installed GPUs on it. The GPUs are most probably Asus Radeon R9 390(X) cards.

Another difficulty of using a server PSU on a GPU mining rig is that in most of the designs you will need to provide power to the server PSU manually by pressing a button, as shown in the picture below. This makes the starting of the rig more problematic especially when the system is intended to run remotely, without direct access and supervision. I do not recommend buying such a configuration as any savings are more than outweighed by the added complexities.

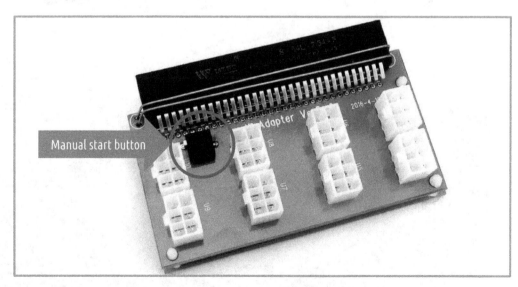

Manual start button

My recommendation is to use a bare chassis or frame or one that comes with PCIE raiser cards. A kit of six PCIE raiser cards usually costs around $50. So, search your local online stores for "mining chassis" or "GPU mining frame".

I found the below picture product on Amazon.com and eBay.com. It is from a website www.degconnect.com, and is made out of wood. It is priced at $135 and has six PCIE raiser cards. But again, you will also need to consider the shipping costs.

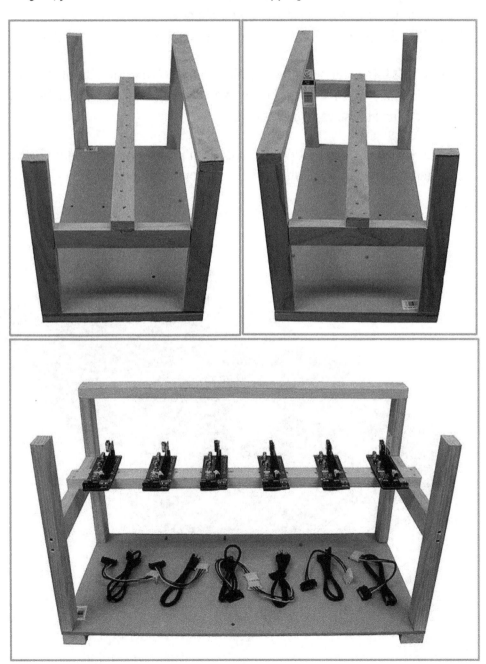

6.4.Make your own Chassis in an hour for cheap

In this section, I'm going to guide you to build your GPU mining chassis with a **shoe rack**. Building a GPU mining chassis of shoe rack is a very common because of:

1. A shoe rack is relatively cheap, usually below ~$50 for a 4-tier show rack, also it is easy to purchase and order.
2. Easily can be assembled and later customized.
3. The dimensions are very close to a perfect fit for a GPU mining chassis.

First let's talk about dimensions. Well, in a normal shoe rack, the distance between each tier is about ~20 cm = ~6" or bigger to accommodate shoes, or sometimes people place flowers, plants and vases on them.

This ~20 cm is adequate to house most of GPUs, for instant Sapphire NITRO+ RX 570 is about 135 mm (5.3") tall while NITRO+ is above medium size GPU.

Figure 3 - Sapphire AMD Radeon RX 570 Nitro+, cooler assembly is larger than GPU bracket.

The width of most of shoe racks are bigger than ~30 cm (12").

Figure 4 - Picture of an ordinary 4-tier shoe rack made of thin metallic tubes and plastic links, each tier has 4 metallic tubes.

Even the largest GPUs barely are longer than ~30 cm (~12"), for instance, ASUS ROG-STRIX RX580 O8G GAMING is 29.8 cm (11.73") long.

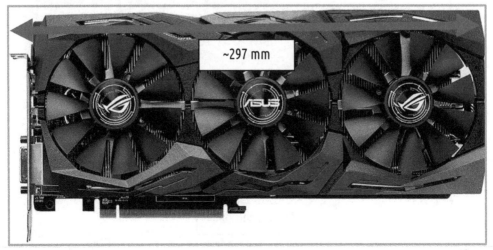

Even if the card is longer than the width of the shoe rack it does not make a big trouble as it may just stay out of the whole rack for few centimeters, while this shoe rack chassis is an open-design chassis and there is no restrictions nor tight places.

About the length of show rack or how wide it should be, well it depends on your build, you need ~10 cm (~4") for each GPU, so for a GPU mining rig with 7 GPUs, your shoe rack should be bigger than 70 cm (~28"). A longer and wider shoe rack is preferable to smaller one, so the size is very important, pay attention to it before you buy one.

There are some **points** you need to put into consideration:

1. Wooden shoe racks are safer than metallic ones, as there is no chance of electrical short-circuit, specially the motherboard is more troublesome, where there are lots of bare connectors at the back of it. Even when you buy a metallic shoe rack never get one that has not been painted or covered.
2. The arrangement of rod, metallic tubes or cube channel of shoe rack is very important, it must be horizontal along with the long side of the rack, that means the rods make a perpendicular angle (90 degree) with the GPUs.
3. The rods should be made a thick metal, because you need to drill some holes for the GPU bracket on it, so holes on weaker tubes get loose easily after few rounds of tightening and untightening.
4. Don't buy those shoe racks that the section and shelf has a preassembled unit, welded or bound together. Why? Because usually GPU heatsink and fan assembly are taller than GPU bracket and holder. So, it makes it very hard to be fixed the on the rack. Also, sometimes you need to fix only two rods instead of four or five.

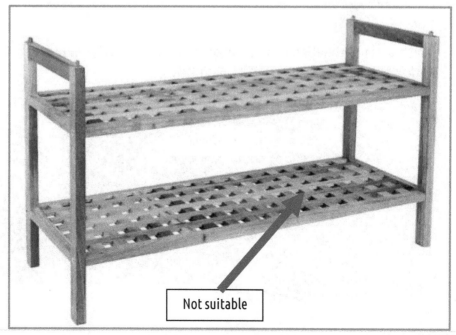

Not suitable

So, let's do it together.

1. place an order for below mentioned shoe rack or similar one from Amazon.de.

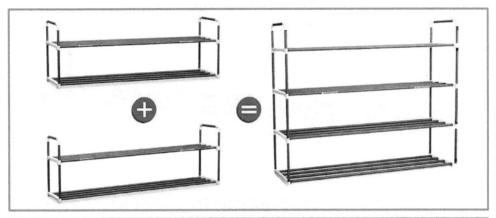

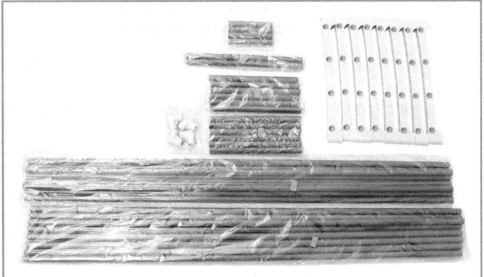

If you live in USA, you may find a shoe rack similar to this on Amazon.com:

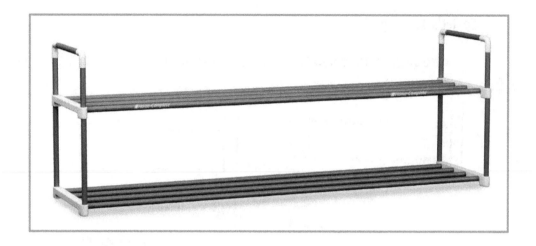

These shoe racks can be purchased about $20 for four-tier types, but don't expect to get something with a very rigid with thick tubes on this price. So, do your own research on the net, or on your local home & kitchen stores to find one.

2. Start to make marks with ~10 cm (4") gap distance on the tubes, rods or wooden strips.
3. Make a mark with a distance of 20.32 mm (0.8") after each previous line .

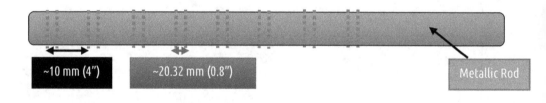

4. Drill two holes on the top on each marked line evenly. Use the drill bit size of 3 mm or smaller. Computer typical case screws have thread diameter of #6 which is defined as 0.1380 inches (3.51 mm).

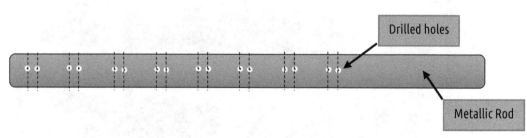

Figure 5 - Picture of parts of a shoe rack

Figure 6 - The tube is marked and drilled

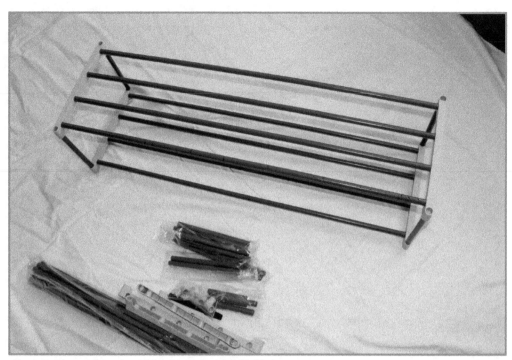

Figure 7 - Picture of two tiers of the shoe rack with drilled holes

Next part is to try a GPU on the chassis to verify your drilling job, if you don't have any, skip this part, go to next section, buy your GPU and come back here. Remember the GPUs are being installed upside-down, in this method, PCIE riser does not have a back support and just fixed on GPU with a small PCIE locking pin. This way suits a build when build dimensions are so accurate, like a home-made condition.

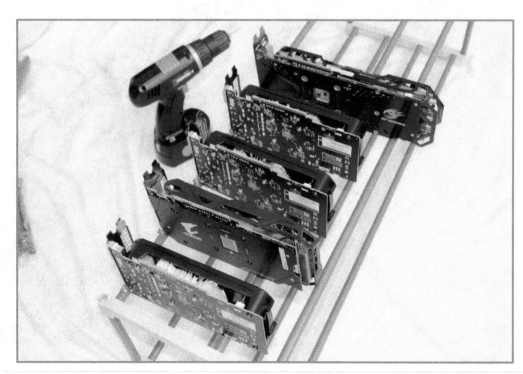

One of top tube was removed to let the card sits on the mountings.

Based on the model of GPU, some has large heatsink and fan assembly, longer than 120mm of GPU bracket, in this case you need to take out the second or third tube of tier basement of to make the card fit and is placed on the rack, as it is shown on the above picture. Always try to get a same brand and model GPUs. It makes it so much easier to build the chassis for them.

5. On next step, you are going to install or stick your motherboard and the PSU on the lower tier. Here, you need lots of double adhesive tape. The easiest way is to cut a piece of thin plywood or similar sheet with size of your motherboard and then stick with double adhesive tape on the sheet, then fix the sheet on the lower tier of shoe rack with double adhesive tape. PSU does not have a bare metal contacts on the outside, so you can directly stick it on the shoe rack.

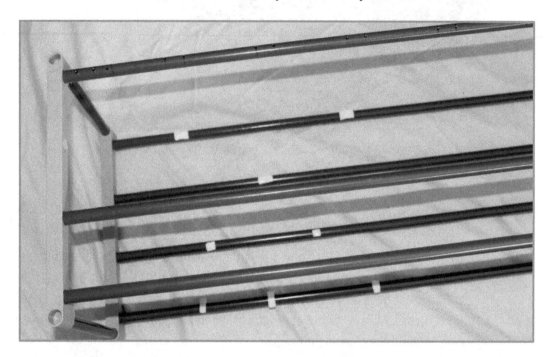

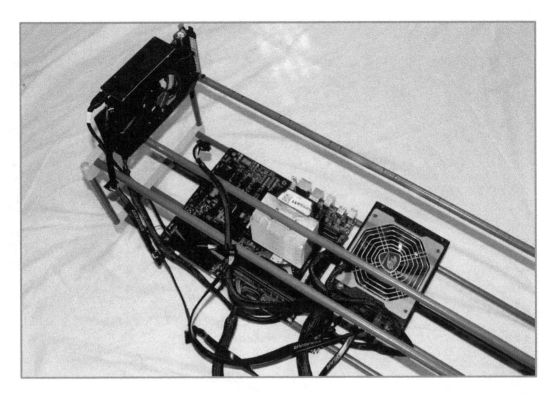

6. On the next step, you can install your GPUs on their places. As I said earlier upside-down, you can fix them upright but you need to build a base for PCIE riser to let GPU with PCIE riser sit on it. While it is possible to do it, but first there is no necessity for it, 2. It makes the build more complicated.

This chassis can accommodate up to 9 GPUs on each tier of shoe rack, so on a 4-tier shoe rack, you can make two complete seven to nine GPUs mining rigs. The total cost of this chassis build was about ~ $50.

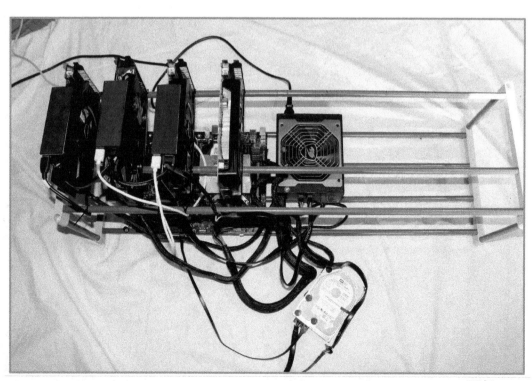

6.5.Get the Graphics card

Remember, try not to mix GPUs brands, model and types. If you go for AMD RX series, get all of your GPUs of mining rig from AMD Radeon RX series, preferably same models and brand, for instant get 6 or 7 units of Radeon RX 570 Sapphire Nitro+ 4GB. The advantages are: 1. Easier installation and integrity in building of GPU chassis, 2. Usually mining software and mining OS doesn't like to have different type of GPUs, may not work at all or very difficult to set up, 3. Performance and temperature monitoring is much easier, you apply in universal clock and temperature settings across are your rigs.

At the beginning of June 2017, while crypto mining was booming, most of AMD RX GPUs were out of stock, started with Radeon 570, then 580 and even 560 4GB version is extremely hard to find. People started to dig again into the Nvidia world and have figured they mine very efficiently despite of initial lower hash performance per dollar of the cards. By end of June 2017, GTX 1060 3GB and 6GB versions are out of stock in most of the markets, and GTX 1050ti had a 20% price jump too from ~$140 to above ~$160. So here once again I bring back the performance per watt chart of Chapter 2 with addition of Nvidia cards.

GPU Showdown						
GPU	TFLOPS	Average Hash Power on Ethereum (MH/s)	TDP (watt)	Hashpower per Watt (higher is better)	Lowest Price	Price/Performance (lower is better)
GTX 1080 8GB	9	25	180	13.9	$ 550.00	22.00
GTX 1060 6GB	4	17	120	14.2	$ 280.00	16.47
GTX 1050ti	2.1	11	75	14.7	$ 140.00	12.73
RX 580 8GB	6.17	23	185	12.4	$ 260.00	11.30
RX 570 4GB	5.1	22	150	14.7	$ 210.00	9.55
RX 560 4GB	2.6	12	75	16.0	$ 125.00	10.42
RX 550 4GB	1.2	6	65	9.2	$ 80.00	13.33
RX 480 4GB	5.8	22	150	14.7	$ 230.00	10.45
RX 470 4GB	4.9	20	120	16.7	$ 190.00	9.50
RX 460 4GB	2.2	10	75	13.3	$ 100.00	10.00
R9 380	3.5	17	190	8.9	$ 183.00	10.76
R9 380X	4	18	190	9.5	$ 217.00	12.06
R9 390	5.1	22	275	8.0	$ 319.00	14.50
R9 390X	5.9	26	275	9.5	$ 355.00	13.65
R9 Nano	8.1	23	175	13.1	$ 523.00	22.74
R9 Fury	7.1	30	275	10.9	$ 355.00	11.83
R9 Fury X	8.6	32	275	11.6	$ 479.00	14.97

Note 1: Average Hash Power is based on the stock core and memory frequencies and voltages.

Note 2: Lowest price refers to a time before GPUs become out of stock on July 2017

6.5.1. AMD GPUs

The best GPU at the moment for a GPU mining rig is AMD Radeon RX 470 4GB. The other option is Radeon RX 570 4GB. However, RX 570 is not optimal, because it has a 5%–10% higher GPU core clock, and a memory clock of 1750 MHz instead of 1650 MHz, which the RX 470 has, but the higher GPU core clock means that it uses more power—the TDP of the card is 150 W, whereas the RX 470 requires 125 W. In real time and under load, the hashing power is around 22-24 MH/s, which is very similar to performance of the RX 470 with stock clocks and around 27 MH/s with overclocked speeds. According to www.1stminingrig.com, AMD Radeon RX 570 consumes 115 W of electrical power with a hashing power of 22 MH/s and 135 W with a hashing power of 27 MH/s when it is overclocked [1]. However, a new Radeon RX 470 4GB is pretty hard to buy while the RX 570 4GB is being sold at the same or lower prices. The Radeon RX 580 is totally out of the mining league because it has very bad power efficiency when compared to the RX 470 and RX 570, even though it can be purchased for a similar price. In June 2017, Radeon Rx 570 4GB was priced at around $200–$250, depending on the brand, shop and availability. Remember:

1. The memory clock frequency rather than GPU core clock frequency is very important for GPU mining performance. All RX 570 cards have memory clocks with a stock memory clock frequency of around 1750 MHz on single channel and 7000 MHz on total quad channel. Few on them have a higher frequency than 7000 MHz.

2. Forget about boost clocks! In a GPU mining rig, your GPU works at stock or lower frequencies most of the time. It does not work on boost clock all of the time. In particular, when the GPU core temperature is above 70 °C you would never see a near close to boost clock when your card works at a normal stock voltage. If you increase the power limit of the card by more than 20% in AMD Crimson software or other GPU manipulation software, you may reach the boost clock but overpowering the card will: 1. increase the power consumption and decrease the power efficiency[1] of the card, and 2. decrease the stability of the mining rig, with the result that the system will tend to crash and freeze more frequently.

So, what should one choose? I stick with those GPUs that have good cooling solutions, and good local support and warranty. And, of course, it all finally comes down to price. GPUs that come with a backplate operate at a lower

---

[1] Read more about power efficiency and performance per watt in previous chapters. In short, efficiency is calculated by dividing the hashing power of a GPU by the power consumption of the graphics card.

temperature and are more robust and durable than those that don't have one. So, when buying GPUs, these are some of the points that you should take into consideration:

1. Always check the local discounts and bargains. Sometimes, online stores such as newegg.com or Amazon offer discounts or rebates which can provide you with some saving on your total build budget.
2. Do not mix different models or brands of the GPUs if at all possible because most of the time, it is very hard to optimize the mining software settings for different GPUs. So, if you decide to use Radeon RX 570, avoid having RX 470s and RX 480s in the same mining rig.

My recommendation is Gigabyte AORUS Radeon™ RX570 4G and Radeon™ RX 570 Gaming 4G, or SAPPHIRE NITRO+ Radeon™ RX 570 4 GB. The stock core clock of RX 570 is around 1200 MHz and the memory clock is 1750 MHz.

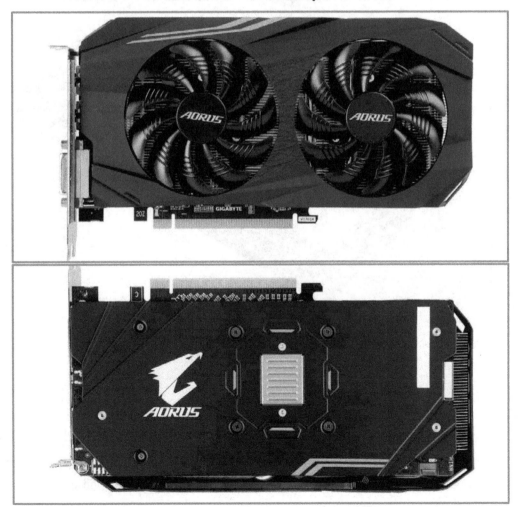

Figure 8 - Picture of Gigabyte AORUS Radeon™ RX570 4G with a solid aluminum backplate.

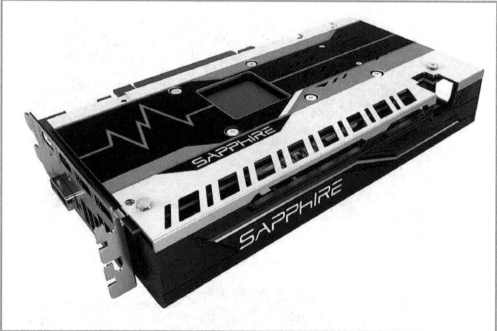

Figure 9 – Picture of SAPPHIRE NITRO+ Radeon™ RX 570 4 GB, with its pretty aluminum backplate.

So, based on your budget, order four to six units of AMD Radeon 570 4GB.

After RX 570 and RX 580 became out of stock in most of markets at the end of June 2017, people turn to RX 560 4GB card for mining. Radeon RX 560 4GB can mine up to 12 MH/s with power consumption of 75W is a good substitute for RX

470. However, the price has gone up in July 2017 from ~ $120 to ~ $150 if it is available to buy!

The problems with RX 560 4GB are:

1. RX 560 4GB requires a single 6-pin PCIE connector so it has similar requirement with RX 570 GPUs.
2. Although RX 560 requires 75W comparing to 125W of RX 570, but a smaller and lower wattage PSU can't be used, why? Because you need PCIE power cables, a low wattage PSU for instant 750W one, does not have more four PCIE power cables.
3. While it occupies a PCIE slot, a six or seven GPU rig with RX 560 is weaker and has less hash power, while the same motherboard, SSD, CPU, RAM, chassis, etc. must be purchased. So, the GPU cost to total cost ratio is worse than the ideal RX 570.

Well, as RX 560 generates less heat, it does not necessarily require a beefy cooler and dual or triple fan. A Single fan cooler works well too.

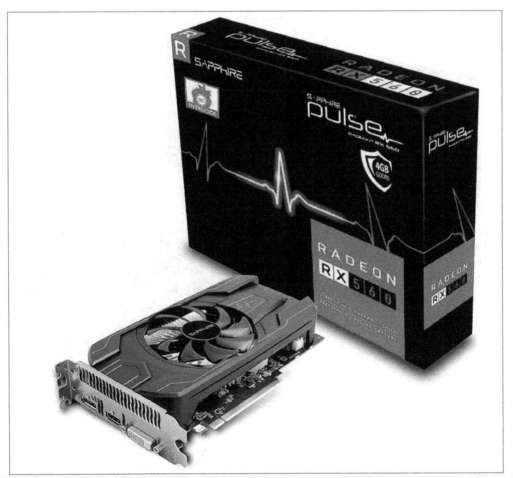

6.5.2. Nvidia GPUs

Well, the Nvidia 10s series GPUs are efficient, as GPU Showdown chart indicates, 1050ti and 1060 stand neck to neck with AMD's. However, they are more expensive relative to the AMD rivals, and not many people would consider them a practical GPU mining option until AMD cards got out of stock in June 2017. Make the long story short, everyone turned to buy 1050ti and 1060 GPUs. GTX 1070 and 1080 are not so attractive because of their selling prices, making them totally undesirable option for a GPU mining rig.

The good thing about Nvidia 10s series card is they overclock very well while being stable too. My MSI Geforce GTX 1060 Aero ITX 6GB card mines ~ 21.60 MH/s with 1000MHz overclock on memory and 100 MHz on GPU core, while the stock clocks are 1759 MHz boost core clock and 8008 MHz memory clock. The temperature stays below 60C with 50% fan speed even with a tiny heatsink and single cooler. On the other hand, you also can decrease the power limit by about 50%, to ~ 80W and still mining rig does not blink once.

However, I don't recommend buying a GTX 1060 3GB card while the memory is not enough for continues mining operation by end of 2017. Besides it has less GPU CUDA cores comparing to 6GB cards, 1152 units to 1280 units.

1050ti is a unique card, the power draw is so low and it does not have a PCIE power connector and it gets all ~ 70W from the PCIE slot. After overclocks and adjusting the power limit, it mines ~12-14 MH/s and draws power of 50W-60W only. This performance, combining with the price of ~150$ makes it extremely efficient for a GPU mining rig, the only remaining problem is occupying one PCIE slot for a GPU, and consequently seven or eight GPU mining rig won't be so powerful. The tricky part with 1050ti is, it would draw all the power it requires through the PCIE riser card, and between 50W-75W is relatively high-power draw from the slot. Power supply of the rig may not support all of the risers, or riser may fail eventually under pressure.

Figure 10 - Zotac Geforce GTX 1050ti Mini with no PCIE power connector

The rest of Nvidia line up, GTX 1070, 1080 and 1080ti don't offer a good performance ratio, specially price to performance ratio. While on the net, some build mining rig based on high-end Nvidia cards, but economically they have much weaker return on investment comparing to smaller brothers.

6.6. Pick a PSU

Look for a power supply with the following properties:

1. A minimum wattage of 1000 W for six units of AMD Radeon RX 570 4GB, where each GPU can use up to 150 W.
2. A PSU that has minimum of six PCIE 8-pin power cables.
3. A PSU with an 80 Plus Gold or higher power efficiency rating. The best price range for such a PSU is around $150 for Gold, and $200 for Platinum.

The best options are:

- EVGA 1000 GQ, 80+ GOLD 1000 W, semi-modular, which is priced at around $120–$150.

- EVGA SuperNOVA 1000 G3, 80 Plus Gold 1000 W, fully-modular, which is priced at around $150.

- Corsair RM1000x, 1000 W, fully-modular power supply, 80+ Gold, which is priced at around $150–$160.
- Corsair HX1000i, 1000 W, fully-modular power supply, 80+ Platinum certified, which is priced at around ~$190.

I always prefer to buy a 1000 W Platinum-grade PSU for around $200 rather than a Gold one for $150. The benefit from the extra $50 is efficiency and one can recover this additional cost over 6 to 12 months from the reduced power consumption (read more in Chapter 4).

The other option is to use a server-grade power supply. The main problems are that: 1. the server type PSUs cannot be used without an adaptor to distribute the output to the GPUs, 2. The PSU of workstations and servers, usually does not supply ATX 24-pin power to the motherboard, so you will require an additional PSU for the motherboard, and 3. usually, they need to be turned on manually or with an extra adaptor to be paired with the PSU of the motherboard.

In general, it is not worth using these PSUs; it is just a consideration in your choice when the price of the total PSU kit is competitive. Such a PSU kit is being sold for ~$90 on eBay.com.

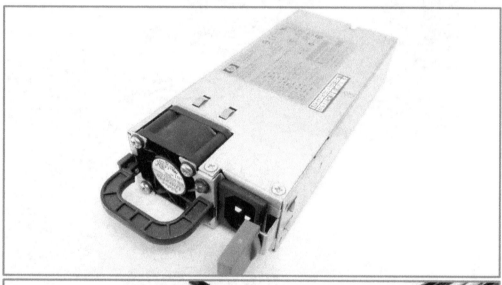

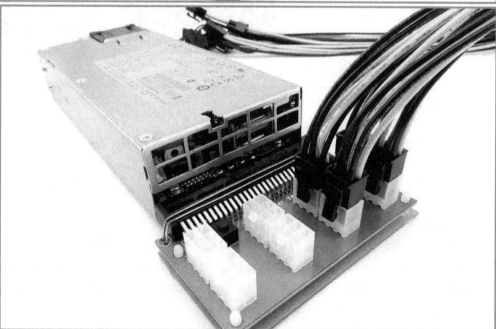

Figure 11 - HP DPS-1200FB A 1200W power supply, with a power splitter adaptor and PCIE power connectors

6.7.Motherboard, CPU and RAM

The best option for a motherboard for GPU mining is Asrock H81 Pro BTC R2.0 which is priced at around $90. The choice of CPU is a low-TDP CPU with an Intel 1150 socket, such as Intel Celeron G1840 Dual Core with price of ~$40. If the GPU mining rig operates in Windows OS, you will require 8 GB of DDR3 RAM; in a Linux-based system, 4 GB is enough. In fact, any DDR3 RAM would work, so aim for the cheaper option.

I have figured that in many online shops Asrock H81 Pro BTC R2.0 is not available and out of stock. The other option of the motherboard is a Biostar motherboard: TB250-BTC which is based on Intel LGA1151 socket. So, it must be paired with intel 1151 socket CPUs and DDR4 rams. For a complete build list please refer to **Ex06-1151-Rev01** example GPU mining rig build in this Chapter and in the Appendix.

6.8.Storage drive

The focus here is on reliability of the storage. As SSDs have the best stability relatively and can be purchased pretty cheaply, my recommendations are:

Silicon Power SP120GB at ~$50; SanDisk SSD PLUS 120GB at ~$55; Kingston Digital 120GB SSDNow UV400 at ~$52.

Spending more $50–$60 is recommended. Note that for most of the time in a pool mining rig (read more about it in Chapter 5), you do not require more than 120 GB of memory.

6.9.Choice of OS

There are two options of OS for a GPU mining rig—Windows and Linux. Setting up a Windows mining rig is easier and should give you more control of the GPU mining software and the GPUs. A Linux-based system requires more technical computer knowledge. However, Windows is not free; it must be purchased and sometimes costs quite a lot while the Linux-based OS is almost free. Furthermore, I have experienced some instability issues in Windows 7 when six GPUs in a mining rig are being used while the same system runs perfectly with Ubuntu 16.10. Recently, a Just-for-Mining Linux-based OS, in which the OS is customized to run mining software without any requirements of installing drivers and other perquisites, has been made available. SMOS from www.simplemining.net and ethOS from www.gpushack.com are examples of these OSs.

On July 2017, SMOS is also has support for Nvidia cards, while offers control over GPU core clocks and memory clocks, it also controls the power limit of the GPUs in watts. So, it is extremely handy in a Nvidia GPU mining rig that require so much overclocking to make the a viable competitor to AMD counterparts.

6.10.   Accessories

You need to remember that most GPU mining chassis or frames do not come with a power on switch, or LED indicators, so you will need at least one power switch. Otherwise, you would have to short the motherboard connections every time with a screw driver or another instrument and this is totally not recommended. The other option is to buy complete switches for the motherboard front panel which does not cost a lot.

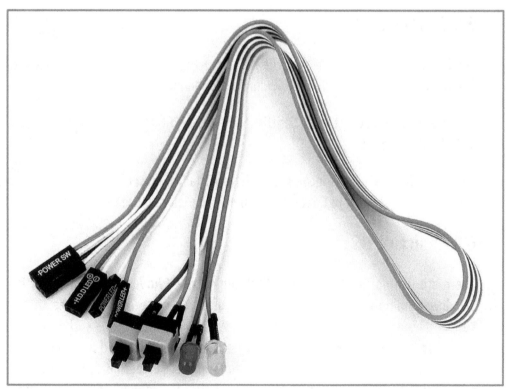

Figure 12 - Picture of Computer Case LED Light ATX Power Supply Reset HDD Switch Cable 50cm from a company is called "uxcell".

The other requirement of a GPU mining rig is the necessary extra cooling. The difficulty is that most typical mining frames do not have a placement or designated frame on which to mount a 120 mm or similar computer fan. It not impossible to fix an extra cooling fan on the frame but installing it is difficult. The easiest way is to glue the fan frames to the chassis with a hot glue gun. The recommended extra air steam is 50–100 CFM per GPU unit (read more about this in Chapters 2, 3 and 5). In a professional mining farm, a complete air-ventilation system should be used rather than local cooling units. Note that computer fans require a fan controller to be able to run, so you will have to take this into consideration.

The other necessary accessory is PCIE riser cards. Some GPU chassis come with a set of PCIE raiser cards, but if you have a bare frame, you will require a complete set and this will set you back ~$50. The recommended type of PCIE riser card use USB3 technology to transfer the data and they are powered by MOLEX power connectors and do not rely on the motherboard PCIE slots.

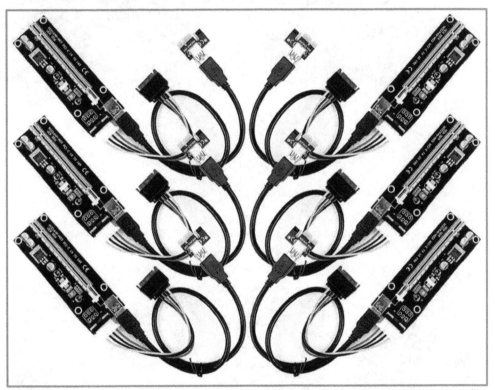

Figure 13 - Picture of a 6-Pack PCI-E 16x to 1x Powered Riser Adapter Card with a 50 cm USB 3.0 Extension Cable & MOLEX to SATA Power Cable.

6.11. Assembling the GPU mining rig

At this stage, you should have all the parts that you will need to assemble your GPU mining rig. Building a GPU mining rig is similar to assembling a desktop computer. So, if you are not confident about doing it, you should seek help or watch some videos online—

there are many guidelines on youtube.com. Search for "assemble a computer" or "build a PC". You will need to make sure the PCIE raiser cards are firmly connected as they don't have a secure mounting place on the chassis. I usually secure them to the motherboard with little hot glue to prevent them becoming loose on the chassis (refer to Chapter 5).

So, your final system should look like the GPU mining rigs shown below:

Figure 14 - Picture of a GPU mining rig with six units of MSI Radeon RX 470, being displayed at www.bitcointalk.org, the link of picture is here!

Figure 15 - Picture of a wooden chassis with six units of Sapphire Nitro RX 480 8GB GPU and a EVGA PSU, the source of picture is a youtube's video from TheBitcoinMiner, link is here!

Figure 16 - Picture a GPU mining rig from www.1stminingrig.com on an aluminum chassis, with six units of Sapphire RX 470 8GB, please visit their website for more information and pictures here!

Table 1 - EX06-1151-Rev01- a sample build of a six GPU mining rig, based on Intel 1151 socket system.

Motherboard	Biostar Motherboard TB250-BTC	$155.00		1	$155.00
CPU	Intel Celeron G3900	$42.00		1	$42.00
RAM	Crucial Ballistix Sport LT 4GB Single DDR4 2400	$33.00		1	$33.00
PSU	Corsair RM1000x	$165.00		1	$165.00
GPU	GIGABYTE Radeon RX 570 GV-RX570GAMING-4GD	$205.00		6	$1,230.00
Case Fan	ARCTIC F12 PWM PST	$6.00		6	$36.00
PCIE Riser	ELEGIANT USB 3.0 PCI-E Express 1x to 16x Extender	$10.00		6	$60.00
Storage	Kingston Digital 120GB SSDNow M.2 SM2280S3G2	$75.00		1	$75.00
OS	Linux UBUNTU 16.04	$0.00		1	$0.00
Chassis	Proper Mining Chassis	$150.00		1	$150.00
			Total =		$1,946.00
			GPU cost/Total =		63%
			(Mobo + CPU + Ram) / Total =		12%

6.12.   Let's start mining

With a Windows-based system, you should have:

1.   Installed and booted Windows 7.
2.   Installed motherboard drivers from Asrock or another manufacturer—it's always better to download the drivers with another computer, onto a USB flash stick and install them though the USB stick, as the Windows generic network drivers do not work with a fresh Windows installation and you don't have access to the internet to download the remaining drivers.
3.   Installed AMD Radeon drivers—the latest are available on the AMD website.
4.   Installed AMD APP SDK v3.0 [2] 64-Bit.
5.   Downloaded and installed a free firewall and antivirus for extra protection of your system—my recommendations are "Immunet" [3] or "Comodo internet security" [4].[2]
6.   Installed MSI Afterburner 4.3.0 or newer version, if you wish to control the fans of the GPUs more easily than with the AMD crimson software. Overclocking is not an option, as I explained earlier in this Chapter. With the MSI Afterburner, you will need to: 1. go to settings; 2. check the "start with Windows" and "start minimized" setting; 3. enable hardware monitoring and control and low level access and drivers, but do not enable voltage overclocking; 4. disable ULPS; 5. click 'okay' and restart the system. After the restart, in the fan section of MSI Afterburner, enable the user fan control, and make your own fan curve. I suggest that you should use the minimum fan speed (i.e. ~20%) until the temperature reaches around 50 °C and the maximum (i.e. ~80%) when the temperature reaches around 90 °C. If it becomes too noisy and the temperature does not exceed 70 °C–75 °C during mining, you may be able to reduce the fan speed to ~60%–70% as long as the temperature does not exceed 90 °C. Later, in MSI Afterburner, lower the power limit by a small margin of 10%, if you are using AMD Radeon RX 470 or RX 480. From experience, I have found that the cards run cooler than 90 °C and the power can be limited by up to 20%, without affecting the mining and hash rate performance. Play with it a little bit to see what works best for you. I personally have not seen any performance improvement by increasing the power limit of the RX 400s series cards.

Now you are ready to start the mining business. I recommend that you use pooled mining. If you are going to mine Ether, you will need a wallet or address to which all

---

[2] If you do GPU mining as a business or professionally, you will require purchasing the business or professional version of antiviruses and firewalls; the free version is only for personal use.

of your earnings can be transfer. There are many ways of generating a wallet. One of the easiest is just go to https://www.myetherwallet.com/ and generate one.

7. Be careful with the password of your wallet. It must be very secure and hard to crack—if you lose it or someone steals it, all your money will be lost. Your password is not recoverable—you don't have the option of emailing somebody or making a phone call to reset it. However, there are ways of making a recoverable account. You can create an account on a third-party website, for instance, that of a broker or cryptocurrency trader, because they usually offer a wide variety of services including your own wallet addresses for different cryptocurrencies. Some of these organizations are Coinbase, Poloniex, etc.

Your ETH address will look like: "0xfc8357AA134980391A14d77EeB6b3288c9a37d71". Your wallet always has a private key. A private key of an Ethereum wallet looks like: "2cd4da6c93457a6764fc73071ff48928151d483fee660fafccf692cfcbde6651".

If someone were to find your private key, they have access to your wallet because a password to get access is not necessary. So be very cautious about storing and using your private keys.

Your wallet address has a graphical representation too in the shape of a QR code. The QR code of the above Ethereum wallet address looks something like this:

The QR code makes it easier in some cases to transfer money—there is no need to type in the whole address, you can just scan it.

In the next stage, you will need to use a mining client to start the actual mining process. My favorite mining clients are **Claymore** and **Ethminer**.

With Claymore, first download the **Claymore** client rev 9.6 or newer version, unpack it into a folder and make a batch file. Change the wallet address to the one that you created beforehand. Your worker name is not important—it's just for identification of your miner especially when you have multiple miners online. Later, you can monitor the status of your miner and the mining performance using the name of your mining, for example, enter "MiningRig01". The email address is optional. The mining client will send you an email if your miner goes offline and it is handy for monitoring purposes.

As the mining commands need to be executed through the command prompt of Windows, you should save your commands in text file with a .bat format to be able to run continuously. Later, you can put your batch file in the start-up folder of Windows to be able to run automatically when the computer is turned on. In Windows 7, go to the "All Programs" menu and then go to "Start up", right click and click on "Open", then paste your file there. Remember to change the running address of the program. You can always find the address when you right click on the mining .exe file and see the properties. Then copy the file location to your batch file.

Ethminer has a similar setup but the execution line is slightly different. Please refer to the website of your mining pool, and go to "help" or "faq" or "how to mine" in order to obtain some guidance on writing a batch file.

When you start the mining client, you may get a notification from your firewall or antivirus about network access allowance. If so, you will need to grant access to it. Also, sometimes the antivirus treats the mining client as a virus. In this case, you will need to unblock this action[3].

8. At the beginning, the mining client starts to upload the DAG file and then execute the pool mining algorithm. You may see some very rapid updates on the status of mining process such as hashrate, GPU fan speed and temperatures. This indicates that your ping or if your PoW and shares have been accepted.

After a while, usually half an hour, you will be able to monitor the performance of your miner on the website of the mining pool. Just go to "stats" or "miner status" section, enter the reference of your Ethereum wallet and see if everything is alright. Some mining pools even offer a prediction of earnings, but this takes time to be completely updated. Usually, you will need to mine for a day to obtain realistic predictions. If you don't see your mining status on the pool website in an hour, there probably is something wrong. Maybe you did not enter your address correctly or you

---

[3] I'm not sure about the reason why antivirus treats the mining client as a threat. During the last 8 months, I have been using Claymore and did not see any abnormality or misuse in my mining rig. Still, you should watch this issue.

are mining using a different server or pool. Always be sure that what you have mined is added to your account.

Based on your mining performance, you will occasionally earn some Ether (ETH), or Etherclassic (ETC). Later, you will be able to cash them for other currencies.

At this stage, you will have become one of the official nodes of the mining network—you will have become a part of the system. Welcome and I wish you all the best.

In a Linux-Bases system

1. Install your flavor of Linux system, preferably Ubuntu 16.04.
2. Update the Ubuntu software to the latest.
3. Install AMDGPU-PRO Driver for Linux following AMD guidelines. The link is here.
4. Restart the system and install the AMD APP Software Development Kit (SDK) v3.0 following the link here.
5. Download the latest Claymore or Etheminer version for Linux.
6. Make your .bash file similar to the Windows setup file and it will look like:

sudo ethdcrminer64 -epool eth-eu1.nanopool.org:9999 -ewal 0xDbbE054e4202FeF68DBaa9864357d9f98eA6F7cB /MyTestRig/youremailaddress@gmail.com -mode 1 -etha 0 -asm 1,1,1,1,1,1 -ethi 8,8,8,8,8 -tt 80 -tt -50,-50,-40,-40,-40,-40 -cclock 1150,1150,1200,1200,1200,1200 -dbg -1 -mclock 1650,1650,1700,1700,1700,1700 -powlim -10,-10,-10,-10,-10,-10

You will need to run .bash file in sudo mode because Ubuntu does not let Claymore miner change the GPU clock or fan settings in non-sudo mode.

Adding -li mode in Claymore decreases the intensity of the mining operation. For instance, my mining with six units of AMD RX 470 4GB can mine 130 MH/s with a power consumption rate of ~850 watts.

If you use: sudo ethdcrminer64 -epool eth-eu1.nanopool.org:9999 -ewal 0xDbbE054e4202FeF68DBaa9864357d9f98eA6F7cB /MyTestRig/youremailaddress@gmail.com -mode 1 -etha 0 -asm 1,1,1,1,1,1 -ethi 7,7,7,7,7,7 -tt 80 -tt -30,-25,-25,-25,-25,-25 -cclock 1000,1000,1000,1000,1000,1000 -dbg -1 -mclock 1650,1650,1700,1700,1700,1700 -li 10,10,10,10,10,10

the hashing power is about 70 MH/s and the power consumption rate is ~500 watts.

```
4 11.993 Mn/s, GPU3 11.713 Mn/s
ETH: 04/16/17-10:17:25 - New job from eth-eu1.nanopool.org:9999
ETH - Total Speed: 70.811 Mh/s, Total Shares: 41, Rejected: 0, Time: 00:49      9
ETH: GPU0 11.381 Mh/s, GPU1 11.713 Mh/s, GPU2 11.978 Mh/s, GPU3 12.037 Mh/s, GPU  t
4 11.987 Mh/s, GPU5 11.715 Mh/s                                                   0
ETH: 04/16/17-10:17:28 - New job from eth-eu1.nanopool.org:9999
ETH - Total Speed: 70.874 Mh/s, Total Shares: 41, Rejected: 0, Time: 00:49
ETH: GPU0 11.406 Mh/s, GPU1 11.726 Mh/s, GPU2 12.045 Mh/s, GPU3 12.007 Mh/s, GPU
4 11.979 Mh/s, GPU5 11.710 Mh/s
ETH: 04/16/17-10:17:32 - New job from eth-eu1.nanopool.org:9999
ETH - Total Speed: 70.893 Mh/s, Total Shares: 41, Rejected: 0, Time: 00:49
ETH: GPU0 11.403 Mh/s, GPU1 11.713 Mh/s, GPU2 12.041 Mh/s, GPU3 11.986 Mh/s, GPU
4 12.037 Mh/s, GPU5 11.713 Mh/s
GPU0 t=71C fan=27%, GPU1 t=48C fan=22%, GPU2 t=53C fan=22%, GPU3 t=46C fan=22%,
GPU4 t=54C fan=22%, GPU5 t=54C fan=22%
ETH: 04/16/17-10:17:46 - New job from eth-eu1.nanopool.org:9999
ETH - Total Speed: 70.806 Mh/s, Total Shares: 41, Rejected: 0, Time: 00:49
ETH: GPU0 11.357 Mh/s, GPU1 11.722 Mh/s, GPU2 11.984 Mh/s, GPU3 11.982 Mh/s, GPU
4 12.035 Mh/s, GPU5 11.727 Mh/s
ETH: 04/16/17-10:18:02 - New job from eth-eu1.nanopool.org:9999
ETH - Total Speed: 70.824 Mh/s, Total Shares: 41, Rejected: 0, Time: 00:49
ETH: GPU0 11.381 Mh/s, GPU1 11.728 Mh/s, GPU2 11.999 Mh/s, GPU3 12.004 Mh/s, GPU
4 11.991 Mh/s, GPU5 11.721 Mh/s
```

With -li 5,5,5,5,5,5, the hashing power is 86 MH/s and the power consumption rate is ~650 watts.

This option is very useful when the GPU mining rig is unstable under some conditions, for example, if it overheats or the GPU core clock is too high.

7. Run the .bash file and enter your system password. Your system should start mining immediately.

6.13.   Introducing SMOS: an easy mining operating system

SMOS is a Linux Ubuntu-based OS, without a graphical interface, but customized to run a GPU mining software. It works best with Claymore mining software. I became acquainted with SMOS about a month ago (April 2017) and since then I've being testing the software. The following are my insights on this customized Ubuntu OS:

1. It is very easy to get a GPU mining rig ready to mine, just by downloading the image of the OS from the website. Use the HDD extractor, which is provided on the website, to unpack it on an SSD, HDD or even stick flash drive. The computer will boot up from the storage drive right away, and directly start the mining program.
2. There is absolutely no requirement to install any drivers or additional software.
3. The mining software is controlled from an online dashboard of the www.simplemining.net website. You may choose different mining clients, such as Claymore, add your wallet information, etc.
4. The software has an automatic updating feature within it. It automatically downloads the update when the mining rig is online.
5. You can customize your GPU settings, underclock, overclock and optimize the parameters of core clock frequency, memory clock and power limits.
6. It does reload the miner program when a new setting is made, or when the miner program crashes or freezes.
7. You can monitor the hash rate power of the mining rig, and the temperatures of the GPU cores.
8. There is a feature that allows you to see the console screen of the mining rig, just exactly as though you have linked your GPU mining rig to a monitor.
9. **The best feature is: it can restart the mining rig when rig crashes or frozen!** This is an absolutely outstanding advantage that I have not experienced even in other Linux OSs. With these, the user must restart the mining rig physically after something has gone wrong during the mining operation.

So, what are the disadvantages?

1. Well, it costs about ~$2 per mining rig for monitoring and operating the software, which is less than 1% of the income from a typical hash rate of 150 MH/s and a six GPU mining rig.
2. I'm not sure how private and secure the system is. The IP address and Ethereum wallet address are made known to the www.simplemining.net server, so you cannot operate the system with perfect anonymity. So, I do not recommend it to those who value their privacy and security. I am not trying to say that your identity would be

compromised or to discredit the beautiful work of www.simplemining.net. However, your IP address and bonded Ethereum address would be made known to any website that you use and open for your wallet, or when you make a transaction. This is not so serious, so this is just a warning that any cloud system that you use would cache your information in the server, including your email address.

By a process of trial and error—changing the parameters of the overclocking section—I found that by letting Radeon RX 570 run at a core clock of 1000 MHz and the memory clock at 2000 MHz, with a power limit at the 2nd or 3rd stages, I was able to obtain the best stable hash rate of 27 MH/s per GPU, and a power consumption rate of 800 W for the whole six-GPU mining rig. So, a mining rig can produce a hash rate of ~160 MH/s and the temperature of GPU core can be maintained at ~65 °C with 40% of the fan speed on Sapphire Nitro+ cards.

References

[1] Ciprian V., 2017, "Are the RX570 and RX580 Profitable? – Mining Performance Review," 1st Min. Rig.

[2] AMD, "APP SDK - A Complete Development Platform," AMD [Online]. Available: http://developer.amd.com/tools-and-sdks/opencl-zone/amd-accelerated-parallel-processing-app-sdk/. [Accessed: 04-Feb-2017].

[3] Immunet, "Immunet AntiVirus" [Online]. Available: http://www.immunet.com/. [Accessed: 04-Feb-2017].

[4] Comodo, "Free Internet Security | Why Comodo Internet Security Suite for PC?," comodo.com [Online]. Available: https://www.comodo.com/home/internet-security/free-internet-security.php. [Accessed: 04-Feb-2017].

7. Appendices

Table 1 – GPU Mining rig: Ex02-1150-Rev01, based on prices of January 2017

Motherboard	ASRock H81 Pro BTC Motherboard	€75.00	1	€75.00
CPU	Intel Celeron G1840	€36.00	1	€36.00
RAM	HyperX 8 GB 1600 MHz CL9 DDR3	€40.00	1	€40.00
PSU	Cougar GX-S 80 Plus Gold - 450 Watt	€70.00	1	€70.00
GPU	PowerColor 4gb Red Devil RX 470	€215.00	2	€430.00
Case Fan	ARCTIC F12 PWM PST	€6.00	4	€24.00
PCIE Riser	ELEGIANT USB 3.0 PCI-E Express 1x to 16x Extender	€10.00	1	€10.00
Storage	Sandisk Ultra Fit – USB flash drive USB 3.0 up to 150 MI	€15.00	1	€15.00
OS	Windows 7 OEM	€25.00	1	€25.00
Chassis	Used wooden cabinet	€15.00	1	€15.00
			Total =	€740.00
			GPU cost/Total =	58%

Table 2 - GPU Mining rig: Ex03-1150-Rev01, based on prices of January 2017

Motherboard	ASRock H81 Pro BTC Motherboard	€75.00	1	€75.00
CPU	Intel Celeron G1840	€36.00	1	€36.00
RAM	HyperX 8 GB 1600 MHz CL9 DDR3	€40.00	1	€40.00
PSU	Cougar GX-S 80 Plus Gold - 450 Watt	€70.00	1	€70.00
GPU	PowerColor 4gb Red Devil RX 470	€215.00	3	€645.00
Case Fan	ARCTIC F12 PWM PST	€6.00	6	€36.00
PCIE Riser	ELEGIANT USB 3.0 PCI-E Express 1x to 16x Extender	€10.00	2	€20.00
Storage	SanDisk SSD Plus 120GB	€45.00	1	€45.00
OS	Windows 7 OEM	€25.00	1	€25.00
Chassis	Used wooden cabinet	€15.00	1	€15.00
			Total =	€1,007.00
			GPU cost/Total =	64%

Table 3 - GPU Mining rig: Ex05-1150-Rev01, based on prices of January 2017

Motherboard	ASRock H81 Pro BTC Motherboard	€75.00	1	€75.00
CPU	Intel Celeron G1840	€36.00	1	€36.00
RAM	HyperX 16 GB 1600 Mhz CL9 DDR3	€60.00	1	€60.00
PSU	Corsair RM1000x	€170.00	1	€170.00
GPU	PowerColor 4gb Red Devil RX 470	€215.00	5	€1,075.00
Case Fan	ARCTIC F12 PWM PST	€6.00	8	€48.00
PCIE Riser	ELEGIANT USB 3.0 PCI-E Express 1x to 16x Extender	€10.00	4	€40.00
Storage	SanDisk SSD Plus 120GB	€45.00	1	€45.00
OS	Windows 7 OEM	€25.00	1	€25.00
Chasis	Used wooden cabinet	€15.00	1	€15.00
			Total =	€1,589.00
			GPU cost/Total =	68%
			(Mobo + CPU + Ram) / Total =	11%

Table 4 - GPU Mining rig: Ex06-1150-Rev01, based on prices of January 2017

Motherboard	ASRock H81 Pro BTC Motherboard	€75.00	1	€75.00
CPU	Intel Celeron G1840	€36.00	1	€36.00
RAM	HyperX 16 GB 1600 Mhz CL9 DDR3	€60.00	1	€60.00
PSU	Corsair RM1000x	€170.00	1	€170.00
GPU	PowerColor 4gb Red Devil RX 470	€215.00	6	€1,290.00
Case Fan	ARCTIC F12 PWM PST	€6.00	12	€72.00
PCIE Riser	ELEGIANT USB 3.0 PCI-E Express 1x to 16x Extender	€10.00	6	€60.00
Storage	SanDisk SSD Plus 120GB	€45.00	1	€45.00
OS	Windows 7 OEM	€25.00	1	€25.00
Chasis	Used wooden cabinet	€15.00	1	€15.00
		Total =		€1,848.00
		GPU cost/Total =		70%
		(Mobo + CPU + Ram) / Total =		9%

Table 5 - GPU Mining rig: Ex07-1150-Rev01, based on prices of January 2017

Motherboard	Fujitsu PRIMERGY RX300 S6	€200.00	1	€200.00
CPU	Xeon L5609	€0.00	2	€0.00
RAM	16 GB 1333 Mhz ECC	€0.00	1	€0.00
PSU	Corsair RM1000x	€170.00	1	€170.00
GPU	PowerColor 4gb Red Devil RX 470	€215.00	7	€1,505.00
Case Fan	ARCTIC F12 PWM PST	€7.00	12	€84.00
PCIE Riser	ELEGIANT USB 3.0 PCI-E Express 1x to 16x Extender	€10.00	7	€70.00
Storage	SanDisk SSD Plus 120GB	€45.00	1	€45.00
OS	Windows 7 OEM	€25.00	1	€25.00
Chasis	Used wooden cabinet	€15.00	1	€15.00
		Total =		€2,114.00
		GPU cost/Total =		71%
		(Mobo + CPU + Ram) / Total =		9%

Table 6 - GPU Mining rig: Ex06-1150-Rev02, based on prices of April 2017

Motherboard	ASRock H81 Pro BTC Motherboard	€75.00	1	€75.00
CPU	Intel Celeron G1840	€36.00	1	€36.00
RAM	HyperX 8 GB 1600 Mhz CL9 DDR3	€35.00	1	€35.00
PSU	Corsair RM1000x	€165.00	1	€165.00
GPU	Gigabyte RX470 G1 Gaming 4GB	€195.00	6	€1,170.00
Case Fan	ARCTIC F12 PWM PST	€6.00	12	€72.00
PCIE Riser	ELEGIANT USB 3.0 PCI-E Express 1x to 16x Extender	€10.00	6	€60.00
Storage	SanDisk SSD Plus 120GB	€45.00	1	€45.00
OS	Linux UBUNTU 16.04	€0.00	1	€0.00
Chasis	Proper Mining Chassis	€100.00	1	€100.00
		Total =		€1,758.00
		GPU cost/Total =		67%
		(Mobo + CPU + Ram) / Total =		8%

Table 7 - GPU Mining rig: Ex07-1151-Rev01, based on prices of June 2017

Motherboard	Asus Prime Z270-A	$160.00	1	$160.00
CPU	Intel Celeron G3900	$42.00	1	$42.00
RAM	Crucial Ballistix Sport LT 4GB Single DDR4 2400	$33.00	1	$33.00
PSU	Rosewill Quark 1200W Full Modular 80+ Platinum	$185.00	1	$185.00
GPU	GIGABYTE Radeon RX 570 GV-RX570GAMING-4GD	$205.00	7	$1,435.00
Case Fan	ARCTIC F12 PWM PST	$6.00	7	$42.00
PCIE Riser	USB 3.0 PCI-E Express 1x to 16x Extender	$10.00	7	$70.00
Storage	Kingston Digital 120GB SSDNow M.2 SM2280S3G2	$75.00	1	$75.00
OS	SMOS Mining OS from www.simplemining.net	$24.00	1	$24.00
Chassis	Proper Mining Chassis	$150.00	1	$150.00
		Total =		**$2,216.00**
		GPU cost/Total =		65%
		(Mobo + CPU + Ram) / Total =		11%
Notes:	1. SMOS cost is $2 per rig per month, so $24 for a rig in a year			

Table 8 – GPU mining rig: Ex07-Z270-Rev01, based on prices of July 2017

Motherboard	Asus Prime Z270-A	$160.00	1	$160.00
CPU	Intel Pentium Kaby Lake G4560	$58.00	1	$58.00
RAM	Crucial Ballistix Sport LT 4GB Single DDR4 2400	$33.00	1	$33.00
PSU	Rosewill Quark 1200W Full Modular 80+ Platinum	$185.00	1	$185.00
GPU	EVGA GeForce GTX 1060 6GB SSC	$299.00	7	$2,093.00
Case Fan	ARCTIC F12 PWM PST	$6.00	0	$0.00
PCIE Riser	USB 3.0 PCI-E Express 1x to 16x Extender	$10.00	7	$70.00
Storage	ADATA Premier SP600 64GB SSD	$50.00	1	$50.00
OS	SMOS Mining OS from www.simplemining.net	$24.00	1	$24.00
Chassis	Proper Mining Chassis can fit 7 to 9 GPUs!	$150.00	1	$150.00
		Total =		**$2,823.00**
		GPU cost/Total =		74%
		(Mobo + CPU + Ram) / Total =		9%
Notes:	1. SMOS cost is $2 per rig per month, so $24 for a rig in a year			

Table 9 - GPU mining rig: Ex07-Z270-Rev02, based on prices of July 2017

Attention: This GPU mining rig may not be stable, the motherboard is not a mining grade, and PCIE risers may not provide enough power to the GPUs through Molex or SATA power cables!

Motherboard	Asus Prime Z270-A	$160.00	1	$160.00
CPU	Intel Pentium Kaby Lake G4560	$42.00	1	$42.00
RAM	Crucial Ballistix Sport LT 4GB Single DDR4 2400	$33.00	1	$33.00
PSU	Rosewill Quark Series 750W 80 Plus Platinum	$105.00	1	$105.00
GPU	EVGA GeForce GTX 1050 Ti SC	$149.00	7	$1,043.00
Case Fan	ARCTIC F12 PWM PST	$6.00	0	$0.00
PCIE Riser	USB 3.0 PCI-E Express 1x to 16x Extender	$10.00	7	$70.00
Storage	ADATA Premier SP600 64GB SSD	$50.00	1	$50.00
OS	SMOS Mining OS from www.simplemining.net	$24.00	1	$24.00
Chassis	Handmade with Shoe Rack	$50.00	1	$50.00
			Total =	**$1,577.00**
			GPU cost/Total =	66%
			(Mobo + CPU + Ram) / Total =	15%
Notes:	1. SMOS cost is $2 per rig per month, so $24 for a rig in a year			

How to deal with generated heat from a GPU mining rig and how to extend the life of the components?

Choose the best GPU for mining Ethereum platform

A complete step-by-step guide to the hardware and software for building a GPU mining rig

What does it mean to mine a cryptocurrency such as Ethereum?

How to start your GPU mining business with only $100?

How much money does a GPU mining rig make?

How to setup a six GPU Ethereum mining rig in 2017?

In-depth Analysis of costs and return on investment of GPU mining business in long-term

This book is written for those people who have little or no idea about the business of mining cryptocurrencies and how to build a GPU mining rig. The reader does not need to have any prior programming or technical scripting knowledge. So, it should be suitable for those who regard themselves as "newbies". I have tried to collect all the ideas on building a GPU mining rig that I have been able to find on the web and I have put the designs in categories, for instance, chassis with open-air or closed-air designs. The advantages and disadvantages of any component or design have been analyzed thoroughly to give the reader as broad a view of the topic as possible.

Recommended Readings

- The Search for Self-Respect by Maxwell Maltz, M.D.

- Psycho-Cybernetics and Self-Fulfillment by Maxwell Maltz, M.D.

- Riches Are Your Right by Joseph Murphy

- The Money Illusion by Irving Fisher

- How To Win Friends And Influence People: A Condensation From The Book by Dale Carnegie

- Praying the Psalms by Thomas Merton

- The Magic of Believing by Claude M. Bristol

- Scientific Advertising by Claude C. Hopkins

- The Law of Success: Using the Power of Spirit to Create Health, Prosperity, and Happiness by Paramahansa Yogananda

Available at www.snowballpublishing.com

CPSIA information can be obtained
at www.ICGtesting.com
Printed in the USA
LVHW101251240521
688332LV00010B/264